WORDSMITHERY

WORDSMITHERY
A Guide to Working at Writing

Robert L. Root, Jr.
Central Michigan University

Macmillan Publishing Company
New York

Maxwell Macmillan Canada
Toronto

Maxwell Macmillan International
New York   Oxford   Singapore   Sydney

Editor: Barbara A. Heinssen
Production Supervisor: Katherine Evancie
Production Manager: Nick Sklitsis
Text Designer: Eileen Burke
Cover Designer: Curtis Tow Graphics

This book was set in Garamond and Zapf Book by Compset Inc.
and was printed and bound by R.R. Donnelley & Sons.
The cover was printed by New England Book Components.

Macmillan Publishing Company
866 Third Avenue, New York, New York 10022

Macmillan Publishing Company is part of
the Maxwell Communication Group of Companies.

Maxwell Macmillan Canada, Inc.
1200 Eglinton Avenue East
Suite 200
Don Mills, Ontario M3C 3N1

Library of Congress Cataloging-in-Publication Data

Root, Robert L.
    Wordsmithery: A guide to working at writing / Robert L. Root, Jr.
        p.   cm.
    Includes bibliographical references and index.
    ISBN 0-02-403541-6 (pbk.)
    1. English language—Rhetoric.   I. Title.
PE1408.R668   1993
808'.042—dc20   93-20316
                                                           CIP

Credit acknowledgments appear on page 142, which constitutes an extension of
the copyright page.

Printing: 1 2 3 4 5 6 7   Year: 4 5 6 7 8 9 0

For Sue,
With gratitude
for shared grace

PREFACE
A Word to the Writer

A preface traditionally is the part of the book that comes before the text and gives the author an opportunity to prepare the reader for what follows. This preface is addressed to the writer rather than to the reader. Whether you start this book thinking of yourself as experienced or inexperienced at writing, you should think of yourself as a writer while you read it. Reading like a writer will connect you more readily to the ideas and strategies presented here and help you become more receptive to the suggestions that you can apply to your own writing—the processes of writing, the attitudes you bring to it, the aspirations you have for it.

Wordsmithery offers explanations and advice to the writer. The book attempts to explain what practiced writers go through to successfully complete any composing tasks they give themselves or are given by others; it shares their writing about writing. Alternative strategies that work for experienced writers are also offered here to help inexperienced writers gain the success and confidence they need to develop into experienced writers. The book is not strictly for a course in composition (although an *Instructor's Manual* is available with suggestions for ways to use it in a composition course); there are no exercises, activities, or assignments. Nonetheless, because I believe that the same strategies that make practiced writers successful will make novice writers mature, the book can serve as a companion to coursework, no matter what the nature of the course. More importantly, it provides a resource beyond coursework for those who can benefit from a little talk with other writers.

Chapter 1 is an overview of what writers have to say not only about composing a text but also about being a wordsmith—a shaper of language, a "forger" of texts; it discusses the ways master wordsmiths work at writing and what novices need to learn to work at it. Chapters 2 through 6 focus separately on the elements of wordsmithery: the uses of writing as engagement with ideas and experience before a text is intended; the preliminaries that help prepare the writer to engage in creating a text; the strategies by which a text can be created; the strategies to revise that text and carry it beyond its original draft; the ways to prepare a text to go public, out into the world beyond the writer's notepad or desk. Chapter 7 returns to the experience of writers by illustrating all the elements of wordsmithery in the work of individual writers; it is the practical counterbalance to the theoretical opening chapter.

A word of caution, which will echo throughout the book: The order of Chapters 2 through 6 should not suggest that composing can be reduced to self-contained units to be arranged in an inflexible sequence. Instead, the chapter order reflects the relative sequence in which these events usually occur, what happens at the center of these activities, and the inexact boundaries that surround them. Although the book may be read in any fashion it pleases the reader—the individual chapters are designed to be consulted and serve as resources independent of one another—the brevity of the book has been deliberate, an attempt to get all the elements of wordsmithery together in a space where they can be encountered in all their interrelatedness, as un-self-contained and nonsequential as they occur in writing itself. Read the first chapter to get the general idea of what happens in writing and what writers need to know; read the middle chapters to see how to put the processes of writing into motion; read the last chapter to see how other writers have gotten through composing. Then put the book aside and write, consulting it for a hint or a strategy of wordsmithery you may need.

My thanks go to the reviewers whose responses helped in the development of *Wordsmithery;* Larry Beason, University of Iowa; Neil Daniel, Texas Christian University; Joe Harris, University of Pittsburgh; Carol Lawson Pippen, Towson State University; Stephen Reid, Colorado State University; Carol Severino, University of Iowa; and Stephen Wilhoit, University of Dayton.

R.L.R., Jr.

CONTENTS

"What I did not realize was that the constant honing of my perceptions and writing ability, the continual practice in trying to express myself, was laying the background for eventual acceptance in a field I had not even begun to explore."

—Sigurd Olson

An overview of the strategies and attitudes that help writers achieve success in their writing.

"It saves and makes available all those years of reading. Otherwise I'd forget everything, and life wouldn't accumulate, but merely pass."

—Annie Dillard

A guide for using writing to build background, store information, rehearse language, and acquire the context for writing.

"Somehow this is necessary to generate the idea—to truly find my direction, even though I may have thought I knew what I was doing and where I was going ahead of time. I need to internalize ideas before I can externalize them."

—Mary Croft

A guide to preliminary strategies for planning and preparing a writing project and assessing its readiness.

"You're learning about the thing you're writing about usually while you're writing about it. The writing of something will make you realize that there're pieces of it you don't get."

—Connie Leas

A guide to strategies for composing a draft of a writing project.

"I find that I can criticize my composition best when I stand at a little distance from it—when I do not see it, for instance."

—Henry D. Thoreau

A guide to reviewing and revising the ideas, organization, and language of a draft.

"I'll have the text as close to perfect as I think I can get it, will think it ready to send. Then the paper copy will expose how awkward and unfinished it is."

—John Jerome

A guide to text preparation and packaging, readying a revised draft for another reader.

7   WORDSMITHS AT WORK   121

"I deem myself to be an experienced writer because I have learned flexibility and the capacity for systematic variability."
                                                                                                  —Elaine P. Maimon

A review of the strategies of wordsmithery through writing samples from work in various stages of progress.

1 WORDSMITHERY:
An Introduction

Wordsmith, the descriptive metaphor for "writer" defined in the *Random House Dictionary of the English Language* simply as "an expert in the use of words," has been chosen as the central term of this book for very specific reasons. It was a term only vaguely familiar to me until, many years ago, Canadian teachers Lorraine Neilsen and Christine Mowat told me they had started Wordsmiths, Inc., and had become writing consultants or "career writers." Their job was to help forge the raw language materials of the workplace into something durable and serviceable. The term has stuck in my mind ever since.

Wordsmithery seems an apt term to me, because it recalls the role of the smith—the blacksmith so essential at fundamental, functional, essential work; the silversmith, so adept at fashioning both items for daily use and items of elegance and beauty that distinctions between craft and art became uncertain; the goldsmith, designing delicate ornaments from precious metal; all of them adjusting the shape of their materials and selecting their resources to meet the demands of the task as well as the needs and interests of their clientele. It also seems appropriate as a metaphor for the writer, because the smith's trade was learned through apprenticeship, trial and error under the supervision of an accomplished artisan, a master in both the sense of supervisor and the sense of teacher. *The American Heritage Dictionary* describes a smith as "one who works metal when it is hot and malleable." The apprentice wordsmith, then, may be imagined as someone sweating over paper-and-ink forges with hot and malleable ideas and words, now fashioning something durable and functional, now designing something delicate and ornamental, all the while striving for accomplishment in the craft of wordsmithery.

The Making of a Wordsmith: Sigurd Olson on Learning to Write

As a writer myself, as someone who has interviewed and analyzed the composing processes of essayists, critics, and business writers, I am always looking for clues about the real world of writing. Once, reading *Songs of the North*, a collection of writings by Sigurd Olson, a popular outdoors author, I was struck by his description of how he became a writer. Olson came to writing fairly late, after growing up with a love for the outdoors, training as a biologist, working as a wilderness guide, and teaching at Ely Junior College in Minnesota. Having read widely in nature writing himself and eventually feeling the need to communicate something about the natural world and his understanding of it through his own writing, he made the transition from teacher-outdoorsman to nature writer.

Sigurd Olson's account of his development as a writer reveals some crucial elements of writing in the real world. For example, Olson's very motivation for becoming a writer arose from his desire to communicate with others about specific subjects; his need to share his experience of the natural world generated his growth as a writer. Describing his years of development, Olson recalled "the gradual growth of facility through endless practice, day after day, the interminable disappointments, and the many false starts" (98). Wordsmiths don't do it right the first time, and they don't achieve their peak levels of performance overnight. Without the possibility of trial and error, it is arguable whether Olson would have ever developed into the writer he became.

The practice Olson mentions consisted of not only genuine attempts to write articles but also daily notes and observations. Olson used writing both to learn writing itself and also to learn nature; his writing consisted at first of taking notes in the field on what I saw and thought about, descriptions of animals, birds, and the countless things observed on each foray into the wilds; until now I had always relied on memory. This was a new activity, and while at first my scribblings were almost incoherent, in time they became more meaningful; but far more important than the actual wrestling with the mechanics of words and sentences was that the very act of recording made me see things more accurately. The longer I tried to recapture scenes and events, the more I saw. (98)

"The very act of recording made me see things more accurately"—for the wordsmith, writing is a mode of learning as well as a mode of communicating, and this use of writing pushed Olson beyond superficial levels of knowing. Eventually, he tells us,

There were times . . . when words and ideas came without effort, and I was conscious of something going on in my mind I had not felt before. Golden moments, because they were rare, it was as though writing generated an energy that tapped new sources of knowledge and awareness. (98)

At such moments in Olson's writing, his language did not simply represent reality as he already understood it, but rather served as a means of coming to know a reality. As composition scholar Kenneth Dowst has observed, "Language in a sense comes between the writer's self and objective reality. . . . [W]e do not know the world immediately; rather we *compose* our knowledge by composing language" (68–70). Through his writing Olson discovered what his understanding of the natural world consisted of. Even if he had never published any of his writing, the writing that he did for himself would have benefited him by expanding his comprehension of the world he lived and worked in.

Moreover, the writing, by preparing the way for his understanding, also prepared the way for his eventual publishing. As he observes,

What I did not realize was that the constant honing of my perceptions and writing ability, the continual practice in trying to express myself, was laying the background for eventual acceptance in a field I had not even begun to explore. (103)

Ultimately, as his dissatisfaction with the work he had been producing led him to expand earlier ideas into the essays that became *The Singing Wilderness*, the book that established his place among nature writers, he discovered "what I had always wanted to say" (107).

Olson's work in progress helped to generate further development both in writing and in understanding. The most deeply held beliefs often of necessity cannot lay easily accessible on the surface; to truly understand them and to discover the language to express them they must be mined, pursued laboriously beneath the surface. Writing not only expresses meaning—it uncovers it.

Furthermore, Olson discovered what *he* wanted to say—not what someone else wanted him to say. His great success as a writer ultimately came from that moment, the moment at which he was satisfying himself above all, whether he satisfied a broader audience or not.

[handwritten margin note: writing for himself is more satisfying, more rewarding in the end.]

The First Element of Wordsmithery: Personal Commitment

Sigurd Olson's description of his development as a writer echoes descriptions by other writers and in some ways encapsulates the elements of wordsmithery. To begin with, *an essential element of composition for wordsmiths is the personal commitment to their writing.* Time and again working writers have said that they write to please themselves first of all. By that, they mean not that they are indifferent to demands made on them by potential readers or the specific occasion for writing, but that they need to accomplish their own goals for a project before worrying whether they have accomplished someone else's. Writers without goals of their own often fail to achieve those set for them by others.

Nancy Sommers, a researcher and teacher, has stressed the importance of students coming "to know what writers know" which is "how to bring their life and their writing together" (30). Bringing life and writing together not only generates personal commitment to writing but also opens the door to understanding any subject matter and helps generate the energy that carries the writer through to a satisfying and successful final draft. As journalist John Jerome writes, boredom "comes from trying to write things that offer no gear teeth for my interest. The most difficult work I know is to write about subjects one is not interested in" (95).

Sue Lorch, an academic writer, has described well the dilemma of writing about something without personal commitment. She tells how, as a college student, she wrote a "one-draft, sure-fire A paper" describing a painting in the college museum and was shocked to receive a failing grade on it. As she struggled unsuccessfully to revise it in hopes of a higher grade, she made a discovery about her own involvement with the assignment and the reasons it had bored her teacher:

> Not for life, love, or sacred honor (a concept intimately tied in my mind with the need to make As) could I conceive of the means whereby I could make my description more interesting. The painting wasn't interesting; it was, after all, of a bunch of cows standing in a nondescript field, and images of pastoral perfection and bucolic bliss did not accord with my view of the world in 1968. As the pile of yellow paper grew deeper, my mood grew darker. I was going to have to take myself to see that so-called art again, through the rain this time, and I didn't want to. I was bored into a near coma by the thing the first time I saw it, and the second time could only be. . . . Whoa. Wait. What had I just said? Had something of *me* inadvertently crept into a paper about a picture? Now I was in deep trouble. Not only did I have to go look at it, I was going to have to become interested in it. (168–169)

In the end she must return to the museum and get interested in the painting—commit herself to active involvement with it—before she can begin to write about it in any meaningful (and academically rewarding) way. Her experience is a common one in college writing, although not all students are lucky enough to get the chance to do the paper over.

Moreover, personal commitment is also important for the development of a wordsmith's voice. Much writing for academic courses is hampered by the writer's attempt to imitate the voices of established writers in the field, to sound like the authors of researched articles and textbooks. A good deal of academic plagia-

rism among students arises from an inability to present researched
information in any other voice—or in any other words—than that
of the original author. Worse, perhaps, a lack of personal commitment often prevents students from finding their own voice
as solidly in their academic writing as in their personal writing.
Even though the voice itself may be an academic voice, a professional voice, a scientific voice, or a conversational voice, shifting
to meet the goals of the writing task and the needs of the writing
audience, if it does not reflect a personal commitment to the subject matter and the writing task, it will be an artificial voice, an
unconvincing voice for the reader, an unsatisfying voice for the
writer.

The Second Element of Wordsmithery:
Immersion in Context

Sigurd Olson's remarks also illustrate *a second element of wordsmithery, immersion in context*. Olson had a subject matter in
which he was deeply engaged—as a student he studied biology
out of personal interest; as a guide he studied the wilderness out
of both curiosity and necessity. His growth did not occur devoid
of context. In the same way business journalist Susan Nykamp, an
excellent writer as a college student, had problems at the sentence level as a beginning staff writer for the Photo Marketing
Association until she learned the photo retailing business thoroughly. Although she had been an outstanding writer in both
English and journalism courses at her university, sometimes in her
early experience as a practicing career writer her lack of background made it difficult for her to take phrases in her notes and
work them into complete sentences—she simply did not know
enough about the subject to have options about what to say
about it. But constant immersion in her field, through conversations with colleagues, reading of professional materials, and continual writing, made her sufficiently assured of her subject matter
to be able to use her writing skills. Her rise to managing editor of
a major publication, *Photo Marketing*, followed the arc of her
growth in understanding of her field.

As researchers in composition and cognition have been telling us, writers cannot consciously juggle all the constraints of writing simultaneously. Carl Bereiter has noted that writers need to attend to written language production, controlled association of ideas, rules of style and mechanics, considerations of audience, aesthetic or critical judgment, and reflective thinking all at the same time. But all of these six skills are sufficiently demanding that consciously concentrating on one distracts from concentrating on others. As an extreme example, someone engaged in calligraphy, the art of graceful penmanship, has to have decided previously what he or she will write; the concentration demanded of calligraphy will not allow separate concentration on meaning. To a lesser extent, all writers face those same kind of constraints. The only way that all of these skills can be competently expressed is if some skills become automatic, so that attention may be focused on fewer constraints at a time. Drafting a story we worry little about penmanship, knowing we can concentrate on it in a later draft, or we ignore spelling and correct forms, knowing we can look them up later; preparing a final draft to submit to an editor, an employer, or a teacher we concentrate on legibility, neatness, and correctness and have difficulty attending to the sense. Similarly some knowledge of subject matter, writing strategies, and sense of audience need to be stored in long-term memory so that short-term memory can deal with limited constraints. It is this immersion in context that stores knowledge of subject matter; philosopher Michael Polanyi calls it the "dwelling in" a particular activity that leads to personal knowledge. As Olson and Nykamp show, in the real world, writing comes from a knowledge base that is neither arbitrary nor transient. In Thoreau's words, "How vain it is to sit down to write when you have not stood up to live."

Where writing arises out of a personal commitment and immersion in context, wordsmiths continually draw on their background. The knowledge they have of their subject matter makes it easier for them to imagine writing projects they might successfully work on and gives them easier access to pertinent information when they need it. Both their learning and their composing are part of the same continual cognitive process. Composition needs a long gestation period, one that begins even before the writer is conscious of being pregnant with intention.

The Third Element of Wordsmithery: Assiduous String-Saving

Connected to immersion in context is *a third element of word-smithery, constant involvement with an area of interest through writing,* what political columnist Tom Wicker has referred to as "assiduous string-saving," a tendency to take note of—and notes on—a range of subjects almost continually. Sigurd Olson models that for us in his copious field notes; columnist Jim Fitzgerald of the *Detroit Free Press* stores items and comments on them in a continually growing and ever-changing folder. In "One Writer's Secrets" Donald Murray advises:

> Keep a planning notebook with you to play in at the office, at home, in the car, on the airplane, . . . while you're watching television, sitting in a parking lot or eating a lonely lunch. . . . [M]ake lists, notes, diagrams, collect the quotes and citations, paste in key articles and references, sketch outlines, draft titles, leads, endings, key paragraphs. (148)

The late naturalist Edwin Way Teale, another notetaker, not only regularly took field notes but also typed them up and dated, titled, and numbered them at the end of each day. Composition scholar Louise Wetherbee Phelps, keeping track of her writing over a three-month period one summer, found that she "talked with family and friends, wrote letters, journals, notes, abstracts, outlines, essays, kept a reading journal, filled three daybooks with notes on my composing, elaborated all these in further notes, annotations and commentary, sketches and maps, drafts, on the computer screen" (245).

Henry David Thoreau, himself an assiduous string-saver, kept so thorough a journal that many critics have pronounced it his greatest work. Certainly it was the source of his major works. Often the journal entries served as Thoreau's zero or rough draft; we can trace specific passages out of *Walden, A Week on the Concord and Merrimack Rivers,* and *The Maine Woods* directly to daily journal entries. His journal was the source of inspiration and expression, the place where he could generate, incubate, and explore the essential ideas of those later works. British novelist Virginia Woolf wrote twenty-six volumes of her diary between 1915 and 1941; Da Vinci, Darwin, Marx, Wittgenstein, Tolstoy, Freud, Emerson, writers and thinkers in every field, have similarly used diaries, notebooks, journals, and logs, and given voice to their most profound insights in the pages of their workaday writing before producing the influential and enduring works by which they are best known.

The Fourth Element of Wordsmithery: Discovery Through Writing

Such interaction with the materials of one's writing is an important occasion for *a fourth element of wordsmithery, the discovery of ideas through writing.* The testimony that writing facilitates discovery has come to us from a multitude of sources, both literary and expository, in the real world of writing. Ideas tend to be vague and unformed until they are put into language, and the groping after language helps writers figure out what they want to say—what they want to mean. Critic Alfred Kazin once observed that "in a very real sense the writer writes in order to teach himself, to understand himself, to satisfy himself" (Murray, *Shoptalk* 38). The poet C. Day Lewis confirmed that impression when he insisted of his own writing:

> I do not sit down at my desk to put into verse something that is already clear in my mind. If it were clear in my mind, I should have no incentive or need to write about it . . . we do not write in order to be understood, we write in order to understand. (Murray, *Shoptalk* 106)

Journals and daybooks are places to discover and rehearse before attempting to draft and revise writing that eventually will go public. Writers in business and the professions find that not only notes but also drafts of memos and other informal communications are occasions for discovery. In college courses written commentary on research and the writing of notes help readers discover what they do not know (or else, in Robert Frost's phrase, to remember "something I didn't know I knew") and prepare them for the later writing they must do to demonstrate their knowledge. Whether in preliminary workaday writing or early drafts, wordsmiths make a place for regular discovery through writing.

The Fifth Element of Wordsmithery: Understanding Composing Processes

A fifth element of wordsmithery is a realistic understanding of the composing process. Wordsmiths have customary work habits, practical expectations about the quality of early drafts, and confidence in their own ability to bring a "professional" text out of a formless mass of materials. Edwin Way Teale expressed this realistic understanding in a letter to fellow naturalist Ann Zwinger:

> I think the reason we dread the first draft of a book so much is not only that it is a time of endless decisions—what to put in, what to leave out, how to begin, how to end, etc., etc.—but it is the time when the book we dreamed of writing, the book that has been floating in the air, so to speak, has to be confined by words on paper. Immediately there are intimations that the book is beginning to be less than we hoped it would be. The reason revision is so much fun is that little by little, day after day, we feel we are lifting the book back nearer the original goal. (Zwinger, xviii)

The discouragement that comes with the first struggle with a draft is one familiar to all writers of books, articles, stories, poems, plays, academic papers, research papers, essay examinations, convention addresses, formal reports, instruction manuals; the assurance that revision will banish that discouragement is something only writers who understand the composing process and who have successfully gotten through it can feel.

Having that confidence does not necessarily make the writing easier. As Teale says of his revision process:

> These are my "Earthworm Days" when I am plowing back and forth through the paragraphs, loosening up lumpy or soggy sentences and enriching the book by inserting new facts and ideas as the earthworm enriches the soil by pulling pieces of leaves under-

ground. Or, to put it another way, I am occupied these days fold-
ing over my manuscript in the sense that Thoreau meant when he
wrote to Ralph Waldo Emerson: "In writing conversation should be
folded over many times thick." (xviii)

Experienced wordsmiths know that writing is hard work, but unlike the apprentice they know the rewards that lie beyond the
labor.

Poet, novelist, and critic Elizabeth Hardwick, while claiming
not to understand why the writing process works as it does,
nonetheless has described how it works: "The brain slowly begins
to function in a different way, to make mysterious connections.
Say, it is Monday, and you write a very bad draft, but if you keep
on trying, on Friday, words, phrases, appear almost unexpect-
edly. I don't know why you can't do it on Monday, or why I can't"
(Plimpton 111). She observes of inexperienced writers that they
often are overly disappointed by their first drafts: "They don't understand that they have merely begun, and that they may be
merely beginning even in the second or third draft" (111).

Wordsmiths also have routines that help them write. Political journalist Richard Reeves, for example, will start writing at five
or five-thirty in the morning and work productively before the
outside world can interrupt him. He knows that his peak period
of energy is early in the day, and he uses that period for the work
he values most (Root 119). In fact, so many writers work on that
kind of schedule that when novelist Kurt Vonnegut attended an
Eastern-bloc writers' conference, almost the first question he was
asked by one of the participants was: "Mr. Vonnegut, what do
you do in the afternoons?" (Root 122–123).

These writers also know that the writing is not likely to be
completed at a single sitting. When Richard Reeves attempted to
write pieces nonstop, he could trace the decline of his energy
through the pages of work; now he routinely breaks down longer
tasks into manageable parts. Many writers have spoken of working regularly in short intervals over a period of time rather than
trying to complete a project in marathon composing sessions.
They settle for ten, five, even two or three pages a day, knowing
that a substantial work will arise gradually. A student writing only
one page for each class day in a typical semester would produce
seventy-five pages by the end of the term or over one hundred

pages if she also wrote one page a day on weekends, the equivalent of ten to fifteen class papers; at a rate of two or three pages a day she would double or triple the equivalent number of papers.

Many writers have testified to the same experience and routinely break down the composing of longer works into short sections or chunks. In addition to recognizing that revision will pull these sections together, they also know that, in fact, the work benefits from this piecemeal approach by extending the time to incubate ideas and to work subconsciously on writing. As Hemingway did, they often leave the work at a point where they know they will have something to get them started again the next day. Such a policy is an antidote to writer's block.

Studies of experienced and novice writers have demonstrated that the strategies for writing that wordsmiths draw on extend to the slightest, most reflexive actions. For example, when experienced writers pause in their drafting, they tend to reread what they have written and let the rereading help generate the next section of prose; inexperienced writers are apt to use those pauses to look out the window or up at the ceiling, as if trying to find the next section floating in the air. The experienced writer knows that the text she produces can help her continue to produce text; the novice thinks the text merely records ideas generated or discovered in an outside world and cannot use the text to help him write.

Comparing Experienced Wordsmiths and Beginning Writers: Some Advice

The testimony of accomplished wordsmiths supports the view that (to paraphrase William Hazlitt): "The more a person writes, the more a person can write." Clearly, the novice in writing can learn a great deal by serving an apprenticeship with such experienced wordsmiths, even if it is only conducted through the pages of a book like this. Moreover, beginning writers can gain by recognizing the elements of wordsmithery and the ways in which their own approaches to writing make it difficult to take advantage of those elements. The contrast between experienced wordsmiths and beginning writers suggests some obvious advice:

- For wordsmiths writing arises out of personal commitment, but for novices too often writing arises out of impersonal assignment and they act in response to tasks imposed on them by others, without a sense of investment or ownership in the writing project. Many problems in student writing arise not from lack of ability or potential but rather from feeling indifferent, apathetic, and disinterested; looking for shortcuts to avoid spending time or energy; and making only a perfunctory, uncommitted effort. Advice to writers: Find a level of personal commitment that allows you to engage yourself in any writing project you face, even ones not of your choosing.
- Wordsmiths live immersed in a context from which they draw inspiration, incentive, ideas, information, and a knowledge of audience and writing plans, but novice writers may be strangers to the context of their writing, lacking knowledge of subject, format, style, strategies, or audience, perhaps lacking interest of their own. Advice to writers: Acquire context in any subject you write about (especially those where your initial knowledge is minimal) not only prior to writing but during writing as well.
- Wordsmiths draw on the assiduous string-saving that makes their experience with the subject virtually an ongoing act of prewriting essential not only for the individual product but also for the act of dwelling in context itself; novices, however, have no stored energy source on which to draw and often engage in jump-start writing, a spark from an outside power source necessary to even get their engines to idle because they have no self-starting ignition. Advice to writers: Become string-savers both in the context of short-term situations (such as a course in which papers might be assigned) and also in the context of long-term situations (such as a career that may frequently ask you to write about your area of expertise).
- Wordsmiths depend on discovery through writing, whether in the workaday writing that constitutes a means of keeping abreast of their own thinking or in the drafting of communicative texts, but novices too often confuse writer-based prose (writing for themselves) with reader-based prose (writing for an audience), continually aiming for one-draft

writing they hope to perform at a single sitting. Advice to writers: Allow yourself opportunities to discover through writing.

- Wordsmiths understand their own writing processes and draw on a range of strategies to focus their attention on what is most important at each moment of each process, but the novice too often assumes that the process is the same for all writers and attempts to follow a prescribed set of activities focused on the final product; by believing that such elements as written language production, controlled association of ideas, rules of usage and mechanics, needs of the reader, critical and aesthetic judgment, and reflective thinking can all be given equal and simultaneous attention, the novice virtually guarantees ineffectiveness at all of them. Advice to writers: Understand the nature of composing, including how others write as well as how you yourself write, so that you can take advantage of its elements and avoid writing episodes in which several constraints are operating simultaneously.

It seems to me that these elements hold true for writing across the board, whether in creative writing, academic writing, or professional writing. The student writer in a composition class is a novice in the same way that a beginner at creative writing might be, and success at writing for both of them may depend on adapting the techniques of the accomplished wordsmith. Regardless of whether the course demands attention to personal subjects and such forms as the essay and the memoir or focuses on academic subjects and such forms as the research paper and the critical analysis, student writers need to have strategies that let them engage the topic on their own terms as well as on terms of the assignment, discover what they know and need to know about the subject and the form of writing it will have to be presented in, produce a draft of the text and work with it until it expresses the appropriate meaning in the appropriate form, and prepare it to go public in a presentation text that will not confuse or distract its reader(s) from its meaning. The student accountant, political scientist, pyschologist, physical therapist, geologist all share these strategies in common with the critic, the technical writer, the business writer, the columnist, the essayist, and the poet.

Although we will continue to draw from the experience and advice of accomplished wordsmiths throughout the chapters that follow, no attempt will be made to turn readers into committed artists; wordsmithery is about art for only a few practitioners—for the rest of us it is a necessary skill in the work we do, the daily accomplishments expected of us in our careers. Barbara Couture and Jone Rymer have made the distinction between two types of writers in the professions: "career writers," those hired for their writing abilities to accomplish specialized writing tasks in the industry, and "professionals who write," those hired for their abilities and expertise in particular disciplines and workplace roles who, nonetheless, are also expected to write frequently as part of their jobs. In the information age in which we live, most professional people will be "professionals who write," and an excellent way to prepare for that stage of a career is to learn effective strategies for composing in the precareer stage that college education provides. The pages that follow will attempt to offer specific suggestions for apprentice wordsmiths, whatever the orientation they bring to their study, in the hopes not so much of their achieving mastery by the end of one slim volume but rather of their inculcating habits of working at writing that will set them on the path to wordsmithery.

2 STRING-SAVING

For the wordsmith in any field, the generation of ideas for writing and the accumulation of knowledge in a topic most often grow out of what Tom Wicker has termed "assiduous string-saving," the constant collection of bits and pieces of information and ideas on a regular basis. String-saving can take any number of forms and is an element in the development of any writer in any field. The most famous example, perhaps, is that of Henry David Thoreau's journal, a work of forty-seven volumes kept over a twenty-four-year period. In it, he recorded and responded to his reading and his experiences, developed drafts of works he later published, and stored field notes on his daily observations. Tracing its progress from his youth to his death, we find in it the full range of his interests as well as evidence of the ways journal keeping aided in the development of his ideas.

Similarly, the string-saving of other writers in other fields has been an important part of their work. Charles Darwin's notebooks on the voyage of the Beagle, in which he recorded observations of plant and animal life, scientific speculations, and encounters with South American cultures, served as the basis for his later writing on the origin of species; Leonardo Da Vinci's notebooks touch on a wide range of subjects, from scientific and philosophical to artistic and literary to personal, and contain drafts of letters, diagrams, sketches, treatises, fables, and jokes. Published texts are available of journals, diaries, and notebooks for a wide range of individuals, including politicians such as George Washington and John Adams, philosophers such as Søren Kierkegaard and Ludwig Wittgenstein, artists Paul Klee and Edgar Degas, dancers Martha Graham and Vaslav Nijinsky, actors David Garrick and Fanny Kemble, psycho-analysts Sigmund Freud and Karen Horney, composers Tchaikovsky and Poulenc, inventor Thomas Edison, religious leaders John Wesley and Brigham Young, naturalists Audubon, Burroughs, and Muir, poets Sylvia Plath and May Sarton, novelists, dramatists, essayists, explorers, revolutionaries—the list is long and varied.

String-Savers at Work

The point, of course, is that these works were not simply compilations of daily trivia, such as meals eaten, hours spent awake, persons met in conversation, although that may be a portion or the whole of some diaries and journals. Rather they were places in which the authors could speculate on the conduct of their own lives and the process of their own thinking, record seemingly random bits of information for further reference, and try out the expression of ideas in a context free of the pressure to prepare a polished text. Virginia Woolf believed that keeping her diary made it easier to do her other writing: essays, reviews, novels. She wrote that

> the habit of writing thus for my own eye only is good practice. It loosens the ligaments. Never mind the misses and stumbles. Going at such a pace as I do I must make the most direct and instant shots at my object, and thus have to lay hands on words, choose them and shoot them with no more pause than is needed to put my pen in the ink. I believe that during the past year I can trace some increase of ease in my professional writing which I attribute to my casual half hours after tea. (13)

The "increase of ease in professional writing" that grows out of daily "casual" writing occurs for most writers who use it; without some sort of string-saving a writer can approach a writing project unprepared both in an understanding of the topic and in a familiarity with the kind of language appropriate to the project. This often happens to writers in the workplace and routinely happens to college writers, particularly freshmen and sophomores taking courses in a wide range of disciplines.

Thoreau was aware of the importance of string-saving as a long-term activity. He once flatly stated, "A journal is a record of experiences and growth, not a preserve of things well done or said" (8:134). The growth comes from making connections that only come about through writing:

> Having by chance recorded a few disconnected thoughts and then brought them into juxtaposition, they suggested a whole new field in which it was possible to labor and to think. Thought begat thought. (3:217)

As Thoreau describes it the value of the journal is twofold: first, to record thoughts, observations, and experiences independent of all other entries, and second, to discover further ideas by noticing and creating connections among the individual entries. In essence, Thoreau is endorsing the view that both comprehension and learning involve connecting new information to knowledge a person already has. Writing is a highly effective way of making those connections.

The travel writer Tobias Schneebaum reinforces this view in an account of his own journal keeping. Like so many travel writers, Schneebaum used his journal extensively while living among primitive tribes in the jungles of Indonesia. He writes,

> My journal was always with me, and I wrote up the day's events as quickly as possible, knowing that even the most important happenings can easily be forgotten. The journal calmed me and forced me to think clearly about the day. Often the day had been muddled with so many things happening one after another that the only way to straighten it out was to write about it, reliving it until the pattern of incidents sorted itself out. Recording specific information had to be done as soon as it was learned. . . . (148–149)

Careful and thorough journal keeping not only recorded specific information but helped Schneebaum to understand it and, later, to connect it to other information he was recording.

Annie Dillard, a poet and essayist, began to keep a journal after college, "finding myself highly trained for taking notes" ("How"

20). In over thirty journal volumes, "all indexed," compiled since she began her journal keeping, she keeps "mostly information in the form of notes on my reading, and to a lesser extent, notes on things I'd seen and heard during the day."

> If I want to write about arctic exploration, say, or star chemistry, or monasticism, I can find masses of pertinent data under that topic. And if I browse I can often find images from other fields that may fit into what I'm writing, if only as metaphor or simile. It's terrific having all these materials handy. It saves and makes available all those years of reading. Otherwise I'd forget everything, and life wouldn't accumulate, but merely pass. (20)

It may be that journals and notebooks record ideas and resources where the writer can retrieve them, but it may also be that the act of recording ideas, experiences, and resources helps the writer retain them better within herself.

The Purposes of String-Saving: Recording, Responding, Rehearsing

As these various writers suggest, the use of string-saving varies with the writer and the writing project. Some writers who draw on their own experiences and observations out in the world use string-saving methods to record and react to whatever they encounter firsthand; other writers who draw on the data collected by others use string-saving methods to record and react to whatever they read; some writers do both. Working on an essay about a trip to Mesa Verde I found myself consulting my journal entries on our travels, brochures, tourbooks, and articles giving me historical background; working on an academic article about a teaching controversy I read widely in what others had written and published about the subject, took copious notes and quotes from them, and consulted my string-saving as I planned my own article. In the first case the casual string-saving I turned to was there because I had kept a journal routinely, with no intention of producing an essay; having written about it in the first place was one of the factors that helped me decide to write about it in a form that could go public and gave me the resources to do the job. In the second case, although I had some background knowledge, I did not have enough to write an academic article and had to do a lot of research and specific task-centered string-saving. In either case the string-saving helped me better understand what I was writing about.

Journals, notebooks, and diaries are not the only means of string-saving. String-saving is a flexible concept that changes shape with the individual—some write things down on file cards and file them meticulously, others jot things on scraps of paper and stick them places haphazardly, still others store items in folders and scrapbooks, and others may use a combination of these. Emerson on a European trip kept one overall journal, separate journals for each country, and a pocket diary for memoranda. College teacher and academic writer Mary Croft has called herself "a file junkie" who saves "ideas, quotations, anecdotes, techniques, suggestions, notes from conference presentations . . . adding to my storehouse keeps me alert, growing, learning" (43–44). The individual writer has to find the method that works best for him. Researchers suggest that various techniques work best for various purposes—for example, to accumulate a broad but superficial knowledge of a topic, note taking is useful, but to gain a narrower but deeper knowledge, journal keeping is more productive. Writers rarely do only one or the other.

The apprentice wordsmith, then, can draw on the experience of the skilled wordsmiths—if experienced writers engage in assiduous string-saving as a routine part of their approach to writing, then inexperienced writers ought to consider ways of string-saving themselves. String-saving serves three purposes: recording, responding, and rehearsing. As a means of *recording,* it preserves resources the writer may want to have available in the future and helps to gather the topic knowledge necessary so a writer can begin to write. As a means of *responding,* string-saving provides a chance for reflexive interaction with ideas and information; the mere act of recording demands some effort at interpreting and drawing conclusions, but it also invites further reactions and discussions in writing that help the writer to understand the subject and to stake out her own position about it. As a means of *rehearsing,* string-saving can serve as a way to practice manipulation of language, ideas, and forms of expression prior to an occasion where actual drafting might begin; such rehearsal frees up the writer's concentration at the time of drafting so that it can be focused on such items as structure and organization or development of portions of the text. Regular occasions of writing for yourself make eventual writing for others easier in the same way that regular occasions of exercise make strenuous physical activity easier when necessary—one does not prepare for the Boston Marathon by watching a lot of television, at least not if one has any hopes of completing the course at all; the same may be said for writing.

Forms of String-Saving

Wordsmiths use a variety of forms of string-saving. Among the most productive are journals; logs; dialectical notebooks; abstracts, summaries, and précis; annotations and marginalia; notes; and books, folders, clipbooks and scrapbooks.

Journals

Journals are made up of frequent entries exploring ideas, recording observations, detailing experiences, and reacting to events. People who keep journals often use them to write about the entire range of their experience, but often journals are focused on specific topics or events, such as a travel journal, a subject-matter journal, or a project journal. Some writers keep more than one going at the same time—perhaps a personal journal for reflecting on daily activities and observations, a place to think by writing, and a response journal recording information from and reaction to reading, a place to record material to be consulted later. Some writers keep a process journal in which they comment on the ideas, progress, and strategies they use for composing a work-in-progress; the process journal is a means of working through to an understanding of the writer's own work habits and composing knowledge. "At age fifty-seven I find myself still learning to work," John Jerome has written.

> Keeping a journal focused on writing matters has taught me more about how to work than anything else I've ever done. I can't say too emphatically how valuable it is to keep a journal, if for nothing else than as a way of examining one's own working methods, for finding out how you can be more productive—and therefore less frustrated. (245)

Some students keep a journal for each course they are taking; others use one journal but make daily entries cumulatively, writing a portion after each class session or composing a thorough rundown of the day's classes at the end of each class day.

Journals usually differ from *diaries* in the sense that a diary is often intended to record the minutiae of daily life as a kind of ongoing historical report about the author written a day at a time, but in practice the two forms often overlap. For the most part they should be spontaneous, impromptu, not an attempt to write crafted, polished prose but rather an attempt to write informal, unmediated prose. Journal entries are most effective when the writer works at an entry long enough to develop ideas and push himself beyond preliminary generalizations. Very brief entries are fine for recording, but they often do not generate connections or allow room for new ideas to develop. I usually advise students in my courses to write for at least twenty-five to thirty minutes, which produces entries two or three pages long; in my own journal keeping I may write for only a few minutes or for a couple of hours, depending on the time available and the subject of the entry.

I use journal entries for many purposes, sometimes to talk over problems I am encountering in my work or in my personal life, sometimes to plan writing I hope to do, sometimes to think through my intentions and strategies in work-in-progress, sometimes just to record where I am and what I am doing. The following journal entry was written July 23, 1979, at the end of the day at the house of friends in Grosse Pointe, Michigan, near Detroit, about a three-hour drive from where I lived. I had picked up a hitchhiker on the way, and in this journal entry I was simply trying to record some of the things I had observed about her and some of the impressions she had made on me.

JOURNAL ENTRY

July 23, 1979

I don't exactly know what made me stop to give her a ride. I don't usually pick up hitchhikers, male or female, partly because of the danger and partly because it's uncomfortable sitting with a stranger. Kathy was in blue jeans, sandals, and a white tee-shirt, her thumb out, a tan soft suitcase stuffed to the top by her feet. I pulled over and watched her run towards me in the rear-view mirror.

She opened the door and stuck in her head, her long red hair blowing across her freckled arms and face. She smiled and asked where I was heading. I explained I was only going as far as Detroit but that was okay and she got in.

I learned some things about her in the half-hour or so that she rode with me. She played jazz piano at the Oakland Center on Wednesday nights; taught or tutored students part-time, on a contract basis, for Oakland University's music department; was disappointed that her sax man's wife kept him from joining her for the weekend. She had hoped to get a job playing piano for the night somewhere. She had $2.35 with her. She had had good rides so far and just hoped no one hassled her, that she got in no hassle she couldn't easily get out of.

She was from Rose City, near Flint. When she saw the Renaissance Center in Detroit, it freaked her out, she said. She said she had to be back on Monday, that usually she was living with some dude and couldn't really have a vacation, that guys she knew went out west and had a good time with hundreds of friends.

When I told her I knew someone at Oakland but hadn't seen him for years she said I should just go sit in his class—it would freak him out.

We talked about vacations, how I hadn't done much. She encouraged me to just take off. She had never been to Canada, didn't know where she was going when she got there. I dropped her at a Total station near the tunnel to Canada, wondering if she would easily get across, wondering what would happen to her.

Most of this entry is information, record keeping, because the experience interested me and I wanted to remember it. The next day when I woke up I realized that our conversation about vacations had struck a nerve in me, that the real reason I wanted to remember it had to do with a contrast I saw between her and me. I added to the journal:

July 24, 1979

I wondered something else while talking to her. I wondered why I at 36 had to wait and worry about finances and all the things I had to get done before I could get away while she at 22 or so could dare the world, unknown, on $2.35. Was I so afraid of life I could not grip it without safety measures all around me?

Had I not recorded my impressions of my hitchhiker, I might not have realized that it was not only her personality that had struck me but also what her approach to life revealed to me about my own approach to life. Often a journal entry does not merely record your experience but brings you further toward understanding it.

Logs

Logs are made up of brief entries recording experiences, responses, and events. A log in nautical use records locations, experiences, and actions of a vessel, almost like a form of bookkeeping. But a log can also be a record of immediate reactions to circumstances and readings, such as a reading log, which accumulates the writer's reactions to assigned or self-chosen texts or a student-teaching log, which records classroom observations and reactions. A writer might record a summary of information gleaned in a specific piece of reading and perhaps note connections with other readings, or he might record the work accomplished that day on a particular project and suggest what work will be done next. In a sense such logs record the progress through intellectual journeys. Logs are often kept in diaries or record books with limited areas for entries. When I use logs in the courses I teach, students use 5″ × 8″ note cards and take from three to ten minutes to complete them, with an injunction to be concrete as much as possible. In the following typical writing log entry a student provides a summary of work-in-progress to record points raised about a draft discussed with other students and to remind herself of where she needs to go next with her revision.

WRITING LOG

In order to revise my paper I will begin by examining the beginning and comparing it to the ending. Then I will have to ask myself whether it (the end) accomplishes my goal. So far, I do not think it quite does. I also need to add more detailed description of what that event in my hometown was like. It seems as though I get a little off the topic by the end of the paper. That, especially, needs to be taken care of.

In a reading log entry another student focuses on an essay she has read outside of class, "At the Buffalo Bill Museum" by Jane Tompkins, and reflects on her reaction to it in regard to her own writing.

READING LOG

The introduction was good. It fed the reader with lots of specific information. This author uses excellent word choices. The words used were easy and descriptive. I liked the way the author displayed examples, events, sights, and exhibits throughout the essay. This helped me visualize what I was reading.

I have problems writing my papers and making sure I have good details! This essay helped me see where to put my details and how to know where to put them. The author in this essay also describes how she feels at times, like on page 222. I feel it's important for a reader to understand the author and her feelings. Like I previously stated, the best part of this essay is the language and the detail the author uses.

Log entries should be as long as they need to be to adequately discuss the information the writer is dealing with; in an independently kept, self-generated log, entries might vary greatly in length.

Dialectical Notebooks

The dialectical notebook is a systematic exploration of the writer's thinking composed of double entries. The writer writes a journal entry on an assigned or self-chosen topic and then reacts to that entry by writing a second entry analyzing the first. Often this is done by making the entries each only a page long and writing them on facing pages. Variations of this technique are called the double-entry notebook and the living journal. In essence this form is dialectical because it creates a give-and-take between two roles—a primary observer and a secondary analyst—played by the same person; it pushes the writer toward a deeper understanding of his response to a specific experience than a single entry would allow him.

Some writers find this approach particularly effective with coursework and research. The first page abstracts, summarizes, or records some aspect of reading the writer has done for the course or for the research project, and the second page analyzes the first page by trying to find another way of expressing its ideas, reacting to the information, connecting the information to other information already collected, or projecting the kind of information the writer still needs to collect in order to understand the subject fully. Particularly where the information is unfamiliar, this kind of approach allows string-savers the opportunity to wrestle with their understanding and expression of the material, to make it their own. This is especially important if, eventually, they are going to have to explain it in more formal writing to others.

Journals, logs, and dialectical notebooks all attempt to create conversations with the self; in the dialectical notebook the second entry extends the conversation from a monologue to a dialogue within the self. It is particularly useful as a way to push the writer to analyze her reflections. Moreover, one need not keep a dialectical notebook per se to use the technique for analysis; any journal entry or log entry can trigger a follow-up response entry.

Abstracts, Summaries, Précis

Abstracts, summaries, and précis are all condensations of specific texts. Writers use them to put ideas in someone else's texts into their own words or forms, in part to record them in a briefer, more accessible format, and in part to learn how to talk about them in terms familiar to the reader doing the abstracting. Particularly with complex, complicated, and unfamiliar ideas, wrestling with words and terms leads to better understanding. A good deal of learning on the job and in the classroom derives from conversations and attempts to manipulate concepts with others. Although abstracts, summaries, and précis can also be formal pieces of writing (abstracts in particular are used in a good many disciplines), employing them as informal pieces of writing serves the writer as a means of conversing with himself about these concepts. Such informal pieces of writing can also serve as journal entries or log entries as well, although they work well when written on note cards, so that they can be sorted out when needed.

Annotations, Marginalia

In the course of reading other people's texts a reader might write comments in the margins or at the beginning or end of the piece, recording reactions, noting structure or lines of argument, making observations about ideas or language or connections to other texts, all of which could be consulted later to jog the reader's memory or to provide a brief guide to the text. Especially in cases where the reader will have to return to the text as a source of analysis or commentary such techniques give more power to the initial reading and help the reader to retain a sense of what has been read. It also helps the reader to interact with the text, helping him to better understand both the reading and his own reaction. Ronald Primeau, in his book *Writing in the Margins: From Annotation to Critical Essay*, gives as an example poet-painter William Blake's annotations of artist Sir Joshua Reynolds's *Discourses*, a published series of lectures on art. Blake's annotation takes the form of a running commentary on Reynolds's discourses, at times agreeing or approving ("True!" "Excellent!" "Good advice!"), at times disagreeing or disapproving ("This is all false & self-contradictory." "Nonsense."), at times commenting and arguing ("Mechanical Excellence is the only Vehicle of Genius." "What is Laying up Materials but Copying?" "Why imitate them at all?") (58–64). By carrying out a one-sided conversation with Reynolds's book through recording his own reactions to its ideas and assertions, Blake is able to interact with his reading and develop his own ideas and assertions.

The importance of interacting with reading should be apparent. Writers often have difficulty writing about a text when they read it through and try to write about it from memory, without having annotated it or without having previously responded to it through some form of string-saving. Even dog-earring pages with particular information or ideas provides a way of retrieving a book's highlights later on, a place to come back to when connecting ideas surface in other reading later on.

Writing in the margins is useful not only in general reading but also in academic research. For example, as part of a project in one of my classes, students were asked to read three encyclopedia articles about armadillos and write up an article of their own based on the information in those sources. One female student began by quickly reading all three articles through to get the feel of them, then rereading each one more carefully, underlining the main idea in each paragraph and writing key terms in the margins so that later she could lay all three articles side by side and notice their similarities and differences by her marginal notes and her underlined or circled quotes. A male student took the approach of simply reading the first article very closely, numbering and labeling each new subtopic in the margin as he went down the page until he had completed the reading and made a thorough annotation of the article. Then he turned to the next article, reading closely again, using the numbers from the first article to note where familiar subtopics appeared, and giving new numbers and labels to new subtopics. He went on to the third article in the same way and then used his numbers and labels to compare data among all three articles. In either case the annotations in the margins helped record the different kinds of subtopics available and helped the writers get an overview of all the information scattered among the three articles. Both could refer back to their marginalia when they began to work on the writing project by organizing outlines to guide the drafting (as we will see in chapter 4).

Notes, Field Notes, Lab Notes

Notes are the record of observations, to be consulted and analyzed later on. The travel writer Vivian Gornick, author of a book on Egypt, tells of "knowing each day I had to get it down, get it down, worry later about what it meant. And thank God I did. If it hadn't been for the extensiveness of those notes. . . ." (Gornick 106). Making notes on the spot, instantaneously, is more likely to preserve information. In an electronic age we sometimes forget to engage information through writing because we do not always receive it that way. Television, radio, telephone answering machines, and tape recorders all transmit information orally and some even record it, but hearing and seeing does not preserve information as reliably as writing. By the same token photocopying preserves text but does not make any one read it. Written notes give the writer something concrete to refer to and forces the writer to become engaged with the information on some level. This is the standard way of preserving new knowledge in the classroom, but the writer too often associates it only with classroom learning instead of with outside learning as well.

Even more useful is the habit of returning to notes and elaborating on them. After Edwin Way Teale made field notes on his outdoor rambles, he came home, typed them up, and cataloged them, giving himself a chance not only to preserve them in a clearer form but also to review and perhaps revise them before he became too distant from the immediate experiences that created them. As with so many of these techniques the act of recording and responding is as important as the actual preservation of the information. Although having notes to refer to is often valuable, sometimes the mere writing of the information helps to preserve it in the writer's memory. Moreover, often the notes help trigger more detailed memories and reflection that the writer might have trouble recalling without some sort of written memory aide.

Commonplace Books, Folders, Clipbooks, Scrapbooks

Some forms of notebooks are used chiefly as storage areas, not only of the writer's own ideas but also of the texts of others. Traditionally a commonplace book was a place to copy passages of interest in other works, perhaps for possible use in quotation later on but chiefly to record ideas of immediate interest regardless of any specific intentions for later use. The philosopher John Locke developed and published a systematic method of producing a commonplace book and indexing it in order to accumulate topics and information to be used in writing. They have been kept by people in many fields. Economist R. H. Tawney's commonplace book recorded comments, conversations, plans of possible books, and observations about political events. Novelist E. M. Forster's commonplace book included quotes from and comments on his

reading as well as copies of his own letters. Thomas Jefferson began a literary commonplace book as a boy and kept it until he
was thirty, recording passages in Greek, Latin, and English from a
variety of poets, dramatists, and philosophers. A clipbook would
be a collection of clippings from newspapers and magazines; file
folders and scrapbooks can be used as commonplace books and
clipbooks. By the same token, those who keep journals often
copy other texts into them. The string-saver saves not only her
own thoughts but those of others as well, because writing doesn't
take place in a vacuum—often it takes the discovery of a new
piece of information or the encounter with someone else's point
of view to trigger connections and start an avalanche of thought
that sorts out or completes half-formed thoughts and ideas.

Approaches to String-Saving

In all these examples the writer attempts to record and react
in circumstances where he is not inhibited by the pressures involved in producing a formal text—worries about format, structure, unity, development, logic, style, or mechanics. These kinds
of regular written engagement with ideas of interest to the writer
help develop both the writer's understanding of the topic and
also the writer's facility with language about the topic. The key elements of string-saving are *informality* and *regularity.* All writers,
no matter how experienced, struggle most with their writing
when they try to deal with topics about which they are unfamiliar
or uncertain or inexperienced and when they write only intermit-
tently, spending long periods without writing anything. Much—
perhaps most—school-based writing that is incoherent or illogical
or banal comes about because student writers have not understood either the topic or their own expression of it. Like experienced writers wrestling with writing after a long layoff, student
writers who only engage in writing infrequently during a semester, perhaps only when a major assignment is due, usually find
writing more arduous and frustrating (and unsuccessful) than those
who write regularly. For both the accomplished wordsmith and the
novice, assiduous string-saving is a way to foster the constant engagement with ideas and language that leads to understanding
and clear expression. String-saving immerses the writer in a con-

text and leads to a better comprehension of the context—a possible end in itself; writing is more rewarding and somewhat less painful if it arises out of a context in which the writer has been immersed.

Clearly then the apprentice wordsmith ought to begin string-saving. Some recommended approaches:

- Set aside time at the beginning or the ending of the day to write for a while in a journal, giving yourself at least twenty to thirty minutes.
- Take time *during* important reading to make notes and time *after* reading to write a response, sitting down to read with an open notepad or a couple of file cards.
- Keep a log focused on a long-term project—a college course, a series of meetings, a number of field trips—in which you react in writing for four or five minutes at the end of each episode as a way of summarizing the events and ideas.
- Take a few minutes before classes or meetings or trips to write about what has happened so far and what is coming up, getting yourself back into the context of the experience.
- Review and flesh out notes frequently, making certain that you understand what your own notes refer to and that you can write complete sentences about the ideas you record, perhaps writing a brief summary of the notes.
- Set up a system of string-saving that seems appropriate to your specific projects and general interests as both a prospective writer and a thinking person. In college courses look for an approach that keeps you engaged with course content and class sessions and helps you record the ideas and rehearse the language of the course. In professional life look for an approach that keeps you acquiring background material, reflecting on your experience, and expressing the language of your field. In personal writing look for an approach that keeps you recording experience, responding to ideas and events, and rehearsing language in your own voice.

Writers with specific projects in mind should begin by using writing to think about the subject and record necessary information, but string-saving should also become a constant act of unspecified preparation for the life beyond the project. A journal or notebook or a daybook should be a constant companion; even bursts of writing at coffee breaks and unexpected occasions can eventually save a lot of string.

For the student writer this may mean knowing in advance what papers need to be written in a course and string-saving for those particular projects, but it also means string-saving for the long haul, for the career beyond the course, the courses beyond the assigned papers. A good many studies of the effects of journal keeping have demonstrated that they are long lasting and deep and pave the way for more expansive thinking and more thorough knowledge. Students who have routinely kept logs, journals, and notes in courses have demonstrated not only greater success with formal writing but also greater overall performance in those courses. At the outset of the semester, at the beginning of each course, some plan for regular string-saving ought to be set in motion, regardless of whether the individual instructor assigns one or not. A few minutes a day of response to a class period, a few lines per each assigned reading, accumulate a wealth of resources over a semester.

3 STARTING

String-saving is a way to be constantly immersed in the context of a topic, a discipline, an academic subject, your daily thoughts and experiences. It keeps you thinking, analyzing, synthesizing, connecting; as a string-saver you are involved in the subject of your string-saving, extending your knowledge, changing its shape. Its primary value for anyone is its ability to promote greater learning and deeper understanding of a topic, a field, or a discipline, and in this regard would be worth doing for its own sake.

String-saving also creates a reservoir of ideas and topic-specific knowledge to draw on when you decide to write. For people who are continuously or repeatedly involved in writing, any writing is a preparation for future writing, even if they have no particular projects in mind when they make entries in journals or record something on note cards or in commonplace books. The same activities that help you learn the subject help you prepare to write about it. Because writing is a means of discovery as well as a means of communication, sometimes the wordsmith discovers a topic or a project through the act of string-saving; projects grow out of connections made on the pages of a journal or ideas juxtaposed in a daybook. At other times a project arises from a request from others to present information or analysis—a memo explaining your position on a subject to a committee on which you serve, a formal report to a board of directors, an assignment in a course you are taking all arise as requests (or demands) from others. In either case, no matter how projects arise, the wordsmith often goes back into earlier string-saving as a way of getting material and looking for connections to aid in an understanding of what is being proposed.

Moreover, composing possibilities can also be explored and advanced through further informal writing used to discover, gather information, generate ideas, speculate, or plan. Such preliminary activities sometimes take place without writing when the topic is the focus of intense mental activity, not only consciously but also subconsciously—perhaps even unconsciously—but most writers are aided in the drafting of a composition by first having written their way through phases of preparation and initiation, no matter how vague or rough that preliminary (pre) writing may be.

The Preliminaries of a Writing Project: One Example

Any one of a thousand ideas bubbling under the surface of your consciousness, simmering in your memory, percolating in your string-saving could eventually erupt into a writing project, but whether self-generated or instigated by others, a writing project usually needs some sort of stimulus to get it in motion. For example, on one occasion my department chair was planning a meeting with English department chairs from other colleges and universities and needed some sort of culminating event to follow a dinner meeting, something informative or thought provoking but also entertaining and enjoyable, because the group would have been meeting all day. He asked me to consider doing a presentation on media and to let him know if I could come up with something. Realizing I had some time to consider what to do and whether I should do it, I pushed it to the back of my mind. Sometimes the ideas in the back of my mind get lost because they do not find anything else to connect with back there and because more urgent ideas—ones I can see connections for—demand more attention and jostle them to the shadows and sidelines.

But as it happened with this suggestion, there was a lot back there to connect to—as my department chair knows, I have written a book and several articles about media and taught several different courses in it over the years. Moreover, one aspect of media had been the subject of conversation among my fellow teachers and me in recent months, because of a concern for visual literacy on the part of agencies accrediting teacher education programs in English. One morning after breakfast, while taking a shower, I started to think up a presentation on visual literacy to present to other department chairs, all of whom would have to wrestle with the issue in their curricula. I remembered some scenes from films based on literature that I use to make my students "visually literate" in my literature and film course, and then I remembered some commercials I have shown in a guest lecture for a friend's class in Broadcasting. I thought of a title, thought of how much I could present in a thirty- to forty-minute time period, thought of the main points I would be trying to make and how those film clips and commercials would illustrate it. After showering and dressing, I went to the computer and typed up a journal entry explaining to myself what I had been thinking about, and then used that as the basis of a memo to my department chair suggesting what I would like to do and inviting his reaction.

Essentially then, I was accepting an assignment to write a lecture about media and checking in with the person who had given the assignment to see if I could take my own approach to it, which would be more rewarding for me, and also to see if my approach met his requirements, which would be more satisfying for him and his audience. The initial impulse does not have to come from me but before I can do it, I need to understand whom I would be addressing, what the occasion for the address would be, what circumstances of presentation length and delivery style I would need to keep in my mind—that is, I need to understand the rhetorical situation that is prompting the project. I also need to know what it would take to do it successfully—what information and examples I have, what ones I would need to acquire, what possible arrangement of information and examples I might pursue, perhaps what I know for certain and what I need to discover; in this case, I know I have a pretty good general idea, some very good specific examples, and only a vague idea of what conclusion I might reach after presenting this information. That is enough to get me started; I know there is a writing project here worth following through on.

Why Preliminaries Matter

Very few writers are adept at finding a topic, generating and gathering information, organizing the content, planning the potential structure, and predrafting a piece of writing entirely in their heads. When the writing appears to come out spontaneously, as it sometimes seems to for some writers, it is usually a result of constant immersion in the topic and long familiarity with the genre or format. Columnists and critics may be dealing with new information or a new focus for their reflections in their columns and reviews, but they do not have to discover simultaneously how to write columns and reviews; business writers may consult new data when they write memos or reports, but they do not have to also research the forms in which they are writing or approach the subject matter as completely unfamiliar material; academic writers usually write up their analyses and conclusions drawn from new data or new perspectives, but they use forms familiar to them from previous papers on similar topics for similar occasions and audiences. In all these cases, familiarity with the kind of writing they want to produce, in terms of both the typical language they use to talk about the subject and the sort of structure they might use, allows them the freedom to focus on ideas. Moreover, familiarity with the subject allows them to focus on specific ideas where they have certain knowledge rather than expend their energy discovering whether they know enough to write on a certain topic. These are the advantages experienced wordsmiths have over apprentices, the kind that come with experience and repetition of similar writing tasks.

Preliminaries are important in composing because they can ease the difficulty inherent in almost any writing project and determine its degree of success. To draw on the metaphor of the writer as wordsmith, preliminaries involve gathering the materials, creating the design to be followed, and discovering goals specific to the project as well as general to all smithery. A smith must know before he sets out the nature of the metal he will be working with, the expectations of the person for whom the artifact will be fashioned, and the condition of his forge, his bellows, his molds, his tools; he must have some knowledge of the design he hopes to follow, the various stages he will need to go through to transform raw material into carefully shaped, crafted, and polished work. Accomplished smithery is not a matter of simply pouring your own molten materials into some universal standard mold prepared by someone else but of creating your own mold to accomplish your own design; it is not firing up a forge and melting lumps of base metal in hopes of coming up with something as you go along and cutting down the work time by eliminating preparation. In all forms of smithery, including word-smithery, avoiding preliminaries only makes the work harder, not easier. To come to the actual drafting well prepared, the word-smith needs to remember a few essential tenets and choose among a range of strategies.

The First Tenet of Preparation: Know Your Reader and Your Requirements

The first tenet is to know who your reader will be and what constraints or requirements you will be under in the final draft you produce. If a writer is writing for herself, she can let the format and the sense of the reader be ruled by her own inclinations and instincts, essentially guided by her own taste; but if she intends to submit her work to a publisher, an editor, a committee of her peers, an employer or supervisor, or a teacher, she would do well to consider what demands of length, format, and design will be made and who the audience will be for the piece she is writing. Some academic writing, for example, is fairly rigid as to structure and design, perhaps requiring discreet sections such as an introduction, description of research design, discussion of results, and conclusion; certain forms of documentation must be used, following specific style sheets and professional manuals such as those prescribed by the Modern Language Association (MLA), American Psychological Association (APA), or other disciplinary groups; certain principles of argumentation and presentation must be adhered to and others avoided. Most writing is done within a generic range—that is, if someone elects to write science fiction, there are limitations on what he can do before the work is no longer science fiction; if someone elects to write for a periodical focusing on theoretical research, there are limitations on what ideas for practical application he will be allowed to present.

Similarly, in classroom situations the nature of the assignment determines the kind and quality of prewriting and drafting that needs to be done. The teacher usually has something specific in mind for the assignment, something she hopes you will learn, some skill you will demonstrate, some knowledge you will display. The topic of the paper has to be related to the topic of the course; the degree to which the paper depends on individual analysis or researched synthesis of others' ideas is likely to be specified in the assignment; there are usually implicit, sometimes explicit, limits on the range of topics and approaches you can take to the assignment. Understanding that a teacher assigning a research paper in a college chemistry class is unlikely to accept unresearched personal reminiscences as fulfilling the assignment is essential information; knowing limitations of length, format, and design helps define the task to be accomplished in the paper.

The information on constraints imposed on the writing task is available in the assignment sheet, the memo requesting the report, the call for manuscripts, or a consultation with the teacher, supervisor, co-worker, or editor. In most cases you can find out what kinds of writing have been done by others along the lines you intend. Teachers often make sample papers available for study so that students can see what has been done for certain assignments in the past; handbooks and style manuals often reprint successful research papers; editors and publishers encourage writers to read their periodicals before submitting their writing, because a familiarity with what has been published gives the potential writer a sense of whether he wants to attempt that form and what is really being asked of him. By the same token, it is a standard observation that a writer should be a reader of the form in which he intends to write. If you have never really read a movie review, you have little likelihood of producing one; if you have never read an academic paper in your discipline, you have no sense of how to produce one.

Moreover, if you only ever produce one example of a specific form of writing, you have little possibility of growing as a writer in that form—and that goes for academic research papers as well as sonnets. Some of the difficulties writers face in academic fields are not only understanding specialized subject matter but also—and at the same time—learning to use the language of the field, write in the voice of its practitioners, and use the formats and genres of specialized texts. Familiarity with the forms you will be writing in and the audiences those forms are directed at makes some of the constraints you face in your writing less constraining.

The Second Tenet: Schedule Sufficient Lead Time

A second tenet is to give yourself plenty of lead time on a writing project. Never try to do things in a hurry with a piece of writing that matters. Overnight wonders only happen when a writer has incubated and planned and rehearsed a piece of writing for a considerable period beforehand; attempts at fast and furious, first-and-final drafts usually give themselves away by their incoherence, shallowness, and disunity. Setting a train of thought in motion allows a long period in which it can gain momentum; things happen subconsciously to the work when it is allowed a period of gestation. In classroom writing, you should try to know as soon as possible what the major writing assignment will be, not because you can get it out of the way sooner—usually an assignment due late in a course has been scheduled for that time to give you a chance to benefit from reading assignments and class discussion before writing—but because an awareness of a task ahead of you gives your subconscious an opportunity to work on the planning and the gathering of materials and, eventually, on the rehearsal of the language you propose to write.

In addition to granting yourself sufficient lead time, you should also develop a time frame or tentative schedule in which to get the writing done. That means breaking down the parts of the project and the stages of the process and scheduling deadlines for accomplishing things. Projects involving research generally take longer than projects drawing on reflection, simply because research usually means examining far more material than the final work will use directly and also because merely accessing data from sources other than your own memory and experience is more time consuming. Developing a time frame also means scheduling periods when you can do the work, particularly if you are not a full-time writer and other aspects of your life intrude on your writing time (demands of your job, your homelife, your other courses). Imagining a concrete schedule helps you decide how much lead time to give yourself. The less certainty you have about what you are going to do and how you are going to do it, the more useful it is to build in time for running up blind alleys and putting yourself in the way of unexpected discoveries. Even when you are confident and secure about your writing plans, it is wise to give yourself more lead time than you might predict you need—often our achievements do not conform to our intentions.

A rudimentary composing schedule would allow time for preliminaries, whatever they may be; for drafting, including additional time for taking care of problems you could not have predicted, which the drafting itself reveals to you; for revising the piece once you are able to see it as a whole (and in spite of the revising you might have done during the drafting); and for preparing the final copy of the text to go public. These are not discreet stages—some portion of any of these activities occurs during most of the others—but trying to attend simultaneously to all of them (and to all of their subactivities as well) simply guarantees giving none of them the attention they need to be successfully, thoroughly completed. Even a relatively short-term project can be scheduled for lead time: if a professor wants an assignment two days from the class in which she announces it, you can still plan and ponder the assignment in a journal entry after class, start a draft that night or the next morning, revise it and prepare the presentation text the second night, and turn it in on time. In the interval between the preliminary writing and the drafting you will be able to gestate much of what goes into that draft.

The Third Tenet: Write Before Drafting

A third tenet is to try to do some preliminary writing before starting to work on an actual draft. All writers use some sort of prewriting to prepare for drafting, whether in string-saving or in particular acts of prewriting; the kind of prewriting you do will depend on the circumstances of your composing. Someone who writes the same kind of piece, of the same length, for the same audience, in the same tone, such as a columnist, may find it necessary only to jot down a few notes or a vague, cursory outline, or to go through an intense period of contemplation; someone who is working in a new form for a new audience on a new subject in unfamiliar circumstances ought to do a great deal of preliminary consideration. In either case prewriting will help make more certain the likelihood that the initial drafting session will be a productive one. People who launch into writing without prewriting generally are at the mercy of their stream of consciousness—whatever connections they uncover or invent as they write determines the direction of their writing, not a bad procedure for a preliminary act of discovery but usually a disastrous one for any attempt at a formal draft.

Having said all of this, I need to add a caution. Just as it can be frustrating to try to write without having done any preliminary work, so it can be counterproductive to think of preliminary work as something that has to be accomplished totally before drafting can begin. Being overprepared is often as troubling as being underprepared—the real goal of preliminaries is to get you prepared sufficiently to work well once you begin. Sometimes the trick is knowing when to stop preparing and start drafting. Gathering materials together and planning the work to be done should give you confidence that the project can be completed, but no amount of preliminary work can cover every contingency that will emerge in the writing; writers need to leave room for discovery and learning to take place during the drafting and revising as well as prior to them and trust in their ability to adjust to them when they occur.

Strategies for Getting Started

A variety of strategies are available for getting started. The following alternatives do not exhaust the possible approaches nor should they be seen as mutually exclusive. Some strategies work better for certain kinds of writing than for others or serve as only one of a number of approaches that a specific project may demand.

String-Saving Review

String-saving often serves, intentionally or unintentionally, as the preliminary writing for specific writing projects. Travel writer and explorer Mary Kingsley, for example, drew on not only her notes and diaries but also on her letters to friends and family for the voluminous information she acquired during the exploring that led to *Travels in West Africa*. Speaking of his first book, another travel writer, Tobias Schneebaum, claimed, "Without my journal to read, without the letters I wrote to friends at the time, I couldn't have done any factual writing" (163). His second book turned out to be a disappointment for him because he had no journals,

> nothing to work from but my memory and a few letters that friends had returned.... For me the book was a disaster ... if I had worked from a journal I might have turned it into something more cohesive, more interesting. At least I would have had a perspective on the writing. (164)

Whether or not you intend your string-saving to be a form of prewriting, when you turn to the development of a subject on which you have written in journal or notes, you often find that a considerable amount of the preliminary work has been done, almost unintentionally, and the subsequent planning and preparing comes more readily.

Rehearsing

Rehearsing is a form of unwritten composition, working ideas in language in your head. It is the imagining of the words you hope to say to start the first conversation with someone you are attracted to, the words you think you will need to say to make your case in a predictable argument, the words you wish you had said during an awkward social situation. Everyone rehearses language all the time; experienced wordsmiths realize that rehearsal can be an aid to writing throughout the composing process—in preliminary work, in drafting, in revising. Mostly this takes the form of writing in one's head while doing something else. Academic writer Mary Croft describes the experience well:

> For shorter pieces I begin by allowing ideas to roil and roll around in my head, usually as I am driving and preferably traveling over familiar roads—like the seven miles between home and the university. This can go on for some time. I try ideas out, looking at them from many angles. I phrase them, rephrase them, discard them, replace them—all the time "hearing" myself talking aloud in my

head. I allow them to play around until the ideas catch and flow, until they have satisfied the inner critic (at least temporarily). Somehow this is necessary to generate the idea—to truly find my direction, even though I may have thought I knew what I was doing and where I was going ahead of time. I need to internalize ideas before I can externalize them. (41–42)

The rehearsal experience—"internalizing ideas before externalizing them"—prepares the way for later rounds of composing; it primes the pump, as it were, so that words flow more easily when the wordsmith sits down to write.

The interior monologue, however formless and spontaneous it might be, can be directed, nudged toward the writing project. Before I spend twenty-five minutes exercising on our cross-country ski machine, I read through notes or journal entries or drafts of work-in-progress, so that I can begin rehearsing my planning, drafting, or revising. Then the interior monologue will continue in the shower or on the drive to school, and when I sit down to write I find I have a lot to say—some writing gets done every time. Writers who do not know about rehearsing are apt to come to a composing session unprepared, unprimed, and sit in front of the typewriter or word processor or hunch over the notepad, waiting for something to happen and growing more anxious about not writing (and making it harder to write by the minute). Journalist John Jerome takes a daily walk for rehearsal time, using it "to get immediately away from work, forgetting about it for ten minutes or so, then letting it roil back up to the surface of the mind. The result, usually, is new insights, new ideas, clearer phrasings. Sometimes I think I use walking as a way of getting away from the writing machine so I can think" (203).

Listing

A simple and direct way to start is to make lists. For example, for an essay about growing up in your hometown, you might list five or six memorable experiences you had, moments that involved you and other people in your community. Or if you know generally an incident you intend to write about, you might list events in the order they happened or list people involved and what each of them were doing. If you are uncertain about the direction you need to go, you might list a series of tasks you need to perform to get the information you need or resolve the uncertainty you feel about the project. The point is to give yourself something to work with. The drama critic Walter Kerr gets started on a review by transcribing and cataloging notes he had written down in the theater, as he watched a performance. Copying the notes over into a more legible form and grouping them under various headings gives him a way of figuring out what he was interested in during the play and, to some extent, it also places him back in the experience (see Figure 3-1). The groupings he discovers by doing this help him figure out the items of information that are most important, both for learning what he thinks and also for planning the order in which he will write about things (Root 138–162).

Cataloging and Segmenting

Another way to get at the material you have or to organize it as you acquire it is to catalog it. John Jerome gets himself going by writing in a journal he keeps on the word processor; he calls it "an electronic notebook," "a rolling memo," "a kind of scratch pad for the day's work." After fifteen minutes or so

> I go through and, using the organizing power of electronic writing, flip the appropriate items into their own files. Moving the various ideas into new places serves a double purpose, because every time I move something out of the journal I review it, rethink where I might possibly use it, and, usually, polish it slightly; I see ways of touching it up, of changing the emphasis or reorganizing it for clarity. I begin to get a new look at what's underneath it. (161–162)

Working on a long magazine article about New Hampshire, he created five electronic files, typing up his notes as he gathered them, then moving them to files on a recent trip, personal memories, New Hampshire history and folklore, physical geography, and the ongoing draft as it develops (51–52). The cataloging helps him organize and review his material; it also helps him put off considering some material until he needs it, allowing him to work on smaller segments.

Segmenting a project gives the writer something more manageable to work with than the entire piece—a section, a chapter,

GEN   — So hard to react. Surprised an empty living r
      — lot of light considering only 2 oil lamps in place ([?]) —
        R bring 1 later —
      — [?]
      — Ghosts grown lightweight in my lifetime —
      — 'I learn of my story'   O to Liv
      — AUD laugh O's description [?]
      — incurable syph, incest, blackmail (refrain from calling Bl
        arson, but I think Ibsen burned that place down) —
      — Light lavender wallpaper, furn not as overstuffed as usual —
      — L was in dining room 'laying out some silverware' when heard
        husband + housemaid (1st Ghost report   O + R)
      — 'Social convention! Do you know I think that's behind all the
        <u>mischief</u> in world today!' L
      — 'What about the truth?'   L
        'What about ideals?' — JN

LIGHT — 'Well we're all descended from such a union' she a coward, not
        true   O sister R — L
      — LV 'All ghosts, our mothers + fathers live on inside of us' L

LANG — 'lots of celebrating, lots intoxicating beverages passing
        around'   Eng
      — 'the more returned, the less' —
      — 'How dare you set yourself against your father?'   JN to R
      — 'Oh, that was when I was a little tie-over'   Eng L
      — W+H 'O is upstairs resting — <u>on a sofa</u>?' L
      — O 'Mother my spirit has been broken, ruined!'
      — O 'Regina is my one hope of salvation!'
      — LV 'Because I'm going to tell them everything' TWICE! before
        interruption, FINE 2nd. AUD laughs CA's-If it wasn't,
        it should have!

FIGURE 3-1. Listing

a scene, a paragraph. As Richard Reeves once put it, describing the creation of a documentary film script: "I can't write a script. No one can write a script. But I can write a scene, and if I write enough scenes, eventually I've finished a script." Thinking about the parts you might productively work on, rather than thinking about the whole, gives you some chance of progress on a writing project and gives the more uncertain segments the opportunity of developing from the discoveries you make in drafting. For longer pieces Mary Croft uses the interior monologue "to discover direction" but then works "in segments, not necessarily in the order in which they will eventually appear," working "from files of material on each segment" (43). In the earlier example of the visual literacy presentation I might choose to work on the scenes from the literature segment or the rhetoric of commercials segment before worrying about the conclusion or the beginning, expecting the completed segments to help me understand what goes into the uncompleted segments and trusting in the revision process to overcome difficulties of overall organization, transitions between segments, and coherence throughout.

Clustering

Clustering is a technique in which you write down a word or phrase in the center of a page, draw a circle around it, and then move outward from it by recording a random series of words and phrases related to it, letting yourself connect things as you think of them. The point is not to organize orderly and attractive clusters but to get as much down on paper as quickly as you can, letting ideas simply come as they come, attaching them to the main circle or to subclusters where appropriate but focusing more on the volume of ideas than the structure. In a sense the network of clusters lays your knowledge of the topic out in front of you and lets you make choices about what to focus on, decide what additional information you need to get, choose what knowledge you have that you can ignore. You are creating something to work with, possibly discovering that only one subcluster makes a worthwhile focus for your paper and feeling free to throw things out rather than force them into your writing plans. The essay, article, or paper that grows out of this approach might focus on a single dense grouping or several branches that seem related in significant ways, whereas branches that seem to trigger few sub-clusters might safely be ignored. (See Figure 3-2 for an example of clustering someone might generate for an essay on growing up; subsets such as those around "the house we lived in" or "adventures" or "Willow Park" actually served as the bases for three different essays.)

Diagrams, Maps, Tables, Graphs, Flowcharts, Grids

One way to work with ideas is to represent them visually. The visual representation can serve as a way to remember the relationships among the parts, but the process of fashioning the image also helps to sort out its relationships. For example, a student assigned to read Mary Shelley's *Frankenstein* might notice that the novel begins with a few chapters written by an ice-bound explorer named Walton, then changes to a story narrated by Victor Frankenstein, which in turn contains a story narrated by the creature Frankenstein had brought to life; the student might then notice that Frankenstein's narrative continues after the creature's ends and that Walton's continues after the death of Frankenstein to the end of the book. Other features of the novel might also capture the student's notice, such the isolation of the narrators, the theme of friendship and companionship, the physical movement of the main characters. In attempting to sort out these elements the student might fashion a diagram (such as Figure 3-3) that helps clarify the relationships among characters, actions, and narratives in the novel. Such a diagram might help sort out the elements that need to be addressed in a critical analysis of the book and help determine what materials ought be included and what discarded in the draft to follow.

Other forms of visual representation perform similar acts of sorting and arranging information, making relationships clearer, presenting a panoramic overview of the project, breaking information down into its component parts, and finding ways of arranging the information for purposes of examination. Mapmaking can stir memories of events in a particular place—my students use maps to start papers on growing up in their hometowns and

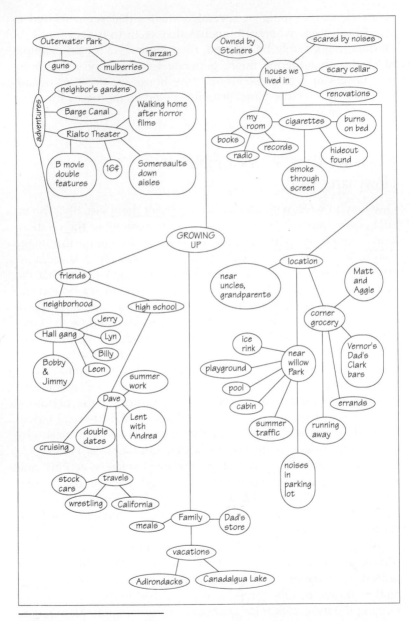

FIGURE 3-2.   Clustering

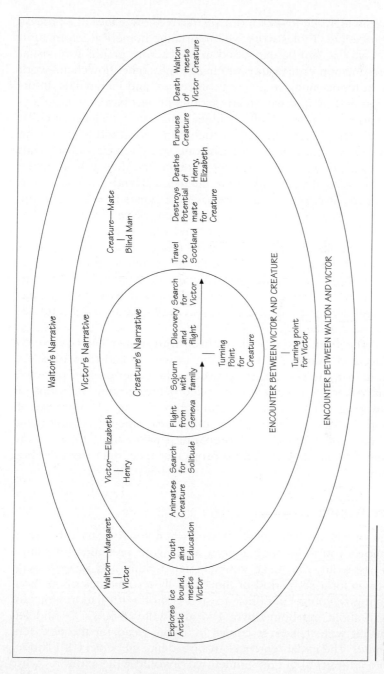

FIGURE 3-3. Diagram

being in high school—or more abstractly show stages in a process or procedure. Tables work well to arrange numerical information and data that can be expressed in brief terms; graphs give visual representation of measures of change over time; flowcharts work best at representing sequences, processes, and hierarchies. Information grids help organize any writing project based on close examination of a series of readings (such as a college research paper). The writer engaged in such a project could begin taking notes on the ideas and evidence one specific source deals with and comparing that with a second source and then a third and so on. To make his inquiry more methodical and systematic, the writer might create a grid composed of boxes in which specific items of information about the topic were placed (see the example in Figure 3-4). Down the left-hand side of the grid would be placed the names of the sources of this information, and across the top of the grid would be the names of the categories of information those sources discuss. This approach helps the writer to identify what is important to a majority of sources and what is important to only a few; it also helps classify the types of information being gathered.

The point is to provide yourself with some means of investigating and examining information in writing and then to select and narrow the portions to be used in the paper or discover what gaps in knowledge need to be filled before writing. As forms of prewriting all these can be useful approaches to making sense of complicated material and giving the writer some way of arranging the parts of a project and preparing smaller units to work on rather than tackling the entire project at once, right from the beginning.

Free Writing

Free writing works particularly well when you feel stuck, because it allows you to be spontaneous about your preliminary writing. To free-write, you make yourself start writing and keep writing *nonstop* for a set period of time, usually ten minutes or so. You might give yourself a phrase to start you off ("If I had to write an essay about my hometown, I would write about . . .") and let yourself write whatever comes into your head for the next ten minutes. The initial sentences may read like gibberish ("If I had to write an essay about my hometown, I would write about . . . who

Title	Structure Organization	Rhetorical Organization	Thematic Organization	Headnotes Focus
Bedford Reader	Rhetorical	Description	Autob, Child, Leis, Self-Disc.	Bio/bib; essay
Compact Reader	Rhetorical	Narration	None	Bio, essay
Critical Reader	Rhetorical	Comparison	Relationships	Bio
Dolphin Reader	Thematic	None	Mortality	None
Eight Modern Essayists	Author	None	None	Bio/biblio
Essay 2	Rhet/Generic	Classic Essays	Nature	Bio/genre; guide
Essay Connection	Rhetorical	Narration	Growing, Family, Nature	Bio, philo, essay
Harvest Reader	Rhetorical	Journ, Autobio.	Family	Bio, intro
In Depth	Author	Comp, Reflect	Autob; Nature	Bio/bib/critical
Inquiring Reader	Rhetorical	Pers. Essay	None	Quote; critical
Invention & Design	Rhetorical	Comparison	Grow; Place; Past; Love; Death	Essay
Lexington Reader	Thematic	Narr; Autobio.	Places	Interpretation
Macmillan Reader	Rhetorical	Description	Fam/Child; Autob; Nat/Sci	Bio/bib; essay
Modern American Prose	Author	Narration	None	Career; style, strategies
Norton Sampler	Rhetorical	Further Read	None	Bio/biblio, essay
Outlooks and Insights	Thematic	Autobiography	Pastimes	Biblio, intro
Prentice Hall Reader	Rhetorical	Narration	Autob, Fam, Nat, Self-Disc	Bio/bib, essay
Read to Write	Process	Narrative	Child/Fam, Humor	Critical
Readings for Writers	Rhetorical	Description	Individual	Bio/biblio, essay
Responsible Reader	Rhetorical	Remembering	Self-Discovery	Bio, essay

FIGURE 3-4. Grid

knows what? I certainly don't, because there's nothing I want to write about, particularly not in that town. After all, that's the place where my sister would have been voted Potato Queen if it hadn't been for . . .") but eventually you find yourself with something more substantive to write. The act of forcing yourself to write nonstop for a set amount of time "frees your writing" by keeping you from having to have something prepared before you write. It helps you find out what is on your mind and avoid the censor or the taskmaster in yourself who sometimes inhibits drafting by being too critical or too anxious about results too early in the writing. From the act of free writing you can discover a topic or a position or a difficulty that will initiate other acts of prewriting.

Looping

The looping technique extends the experience of free writing by "looping" back to something in your initial writing to surface as the focus for the next round of free writing ("My sister being cheated out of the Potato Queen title really made us all angry with the community; I even did some vandalism to get even with them, because . . ."). Additional rounds, if necessary, continually start with some small part of the previous loop ("When I smashed the mayor's front window because my sister did not get the Potato Queen crown, it summed up my anger against the town . . ."). Many inexperienced writers start a piece of writing far too generally or broadly to sustain the draft they intend; the paper never really gets down to the "real" subject before the writer runs out of steam. Looping is one way of focusing before drafting.

Conversation and Brainstorming

Talking things over with others gives you the advantages of other perspectives and the need to clarify what you mean. Conversation is often exploratory, people not so much explaining their positions as discovering them in the process of explaining them. A good listener who asks interested questions helps the speaker dig deeper. In the same way a brainstorming session in which people bounce ideas off of one another has the advantage of sparking connections—someone else's idea reminds you of something you might not have recalled or helps you understand your attitudes better. Students trying to get a grasp on the requirements of an assignment can particularly benefit from brainstorming, because it helps them discover a range of ideas they might not recognize on their own. Sometimes students can benefit from talking to their teachers, not so much because teachers can advise them about the potential of their work-in-progress (which they can) but more because the simple act of trying to put ideas into words helps clarify them. A good many writers have learned to interact with others as a way of working through plans and problems in their writing. Sometimes the interaction takes the form of writing groups, where people meet to discuss one another's work-in-progress, an idea that is often adopted in classrooms but too often avoided by students outside of the classroom; study groups meeting to discuss coursework might be even more productive if they were to discuss assignments-in-progress as well. But primarily what the writer needs is a sympathetic sounding board giving her the opportunity to work actively on her writing through language.

Unsent Letters

Like journal entries, unsent letters are a way of discussing work-in-progress informally, and also like journal entries, they help at any stage of writing. The idea is simply to start a letter to someone you know explaining what you are working on, what you hope to accomplish, and what problems you are having that you need to resolve. This helps to clarify the work-in-progress by giving you an informal occasion and a sympathetic reader and reducing the stress of producing something formally. In the end you do not bother to send the letter but use its insights in planning the draft of the work. Sometimes portions of the letter end up as portions of the work-in-progress.

Zero or Discovery Drafts

Zero drafts are forms of the paper that are carried out before the rough draft or first draft—that is, before you are really making much of an attempt to take formal control of the paper; they are also called discovery drafts, because you write them simply to give yourself some sense of what you might say about the topic you have chosen (or had chosen for you—these prewriting techniques are particularly effective with academic assignments imposed on student writers). Even if you do not keep a journal or a dialectical notebook or the like, you can write a zero or discovery draft simply to find out what you know and how you might talk about it. The zero draft works most productively on writing projects that depend on your prior knowledge, material that can be drawn from experience or memory, because it helps discover problems of organization as well as usable material; it works less well with research writing projects because you may initially have less prior knowledge to discover or organize. In practice, a writer who starts a draft before he is really ready may end up producing a zero draft without intending to. The trick then is to recognize that this draft has simply provided a base from which to begin planning (and prewriting) ways of writing a new first draft that is more on track.

Starting an Essay: One Example

As a follow-up to these ideas, consider the following example of preliminary work on a writing project. A local newspaper had a Sunday column called "Our Place, and Yours," which was composed chiefly of pieces sent in by readers. In a class I was teaching I assigned my students to write for the column and helped prepare them by giving them reprints of several columns, reading and discussing them in class, and pointing out the requirement that the piece be no more than 450 words long. We considered the kinds of stories the paper was publishing, talked in small groups about ideas for the column, wrote journal entries about them, and shared drafts in class. I decided to write along with my students; in thinking about possible topics that would be appropriate for the column I remembered my reaction to the hitchhiker I had picked up four years earlier and went into my journal to find the entries about her (reprinted in chapter 2). To get me started on the drafting I wrote the following in longhand:

DISCOVERY DRAFT

Learning from a Hitchhiker

For years most of my travels had been business, driving to meetings or conventions, usually alone. It seemed odd to be going off to Detroit to spend a night with friends just for the fun of it. Without that destination in mind, I would simply have spent the weekend in my apartment, writing and grading papers.

Now I was speeding down Interstate 75 in the middle of a Saturday morning, talking to the red-headed hitchhiker I'd picked up just south of Flint. We both had Oakland University connections. I told her a college friend I hadn't seen for thirteen years was teaching there. She said I should drop down and just go sit in his class—it would freak him out. She laughed warmly imagining it. Then we talked about her travels.

She was on her way to Canada for the weekend, eager to get away although she had to be back on Monday. "Usually I'm living with some dude and can't really have a vacation," she said. "A friend of mine was going to go with me this weekend but his wife wouldn't let him. It's really a bummer." I nodded sympathetically and asked where she was going in Canada. She didn't know and somehow it came out that she was traveling on two dollars and thirty-five cents.

"Wait a minute, how can you afford to go to Canada on $2.35?"

"Maybe I'll get a gig in Windsor tonight playing piano." She shrugged. "Something will turn up. I just hope nobody hassles me. Usually nobody does."

A part of me inwardly dismissed her as a likable but flaky counter-culture type, but part of me who hadn't taken any vacation in at least four years was challenged. I wondered why I at age 36 had to wait and worry about finances and busywork and attention to unrewarding responsibilities while she at 22 or so could dare the world, unprepared, on $2.35. Perhaps she was foolhardy, but was I so afraid of life that I couldn't reach out for it without safety measures all around me?

When she saw the RenCen, she said it freaked her out. I dropped her near the tunnel to Canada, neither of us certain that she could cross there. I don't know if she made it back from Canada or not, but I know that two weeks later I was camping alone in the Leelanau Peninsula, all my obligations left behind for a weekend. I went to Sleeping Bear Dunes. It freaked me out.

When I read it through later I realized that some words and phrases in my journal entry had been used in the draft and that certain ideas—the sense of her personality, the idea of my not having vacationed and then going off on my own inspired by her example—and certain language had been important to get into the text. But I also realized that it was crammed with information and that it announced its theme rather than revealed it by the details of conversation and events. The draft might have been a rough draft or a first draft, but I decided to come at the telling a different way, by starting a whole new draft from scratch. This was a zero draft, a discovery draft, a writer-based draft that had revealed to me a number of things that were important to me about this experience but that no amount of revising would make into the text I hoped for. I had to start over, but I had a better sense of where to start from having done this preliminary work.

The Importance of Preliminary Strategies for Drafting

Some preliminary strategies are chiefly ways to gather information, others are ways to focus on ideas. It helps to have a full repertoire of prewriting techniques to draw on as you need them and to use them to serve your own ends. Some work better for material you are detached from, such as the research for a typical term paper, and others work best for projects where you need to get in touch with what you have already stored away. In some cases you may even want to try two or three strategies on the same project—for example, clustering to give yourself ideas and then free writing to get into a more focused analysis. The point is to be able to get yourself started and to have some solid sense of what you are doing or what you can expect once you start drafting. Getting something on paper begins to clarify and define the work-in-progress and prepares the way for productive drafting sessions.

Depending on the writing occasion and project, the kinds of prewriting discussed here may be sufficient to produce a sense of where to start and where to go after you start. If the work is short enough, simple enough, or thoroughly rehearsed, and if the format and audience are familiar, it is possible to begin drafting and trust in the text you produce to generate the text you need to produce, more or less spontaneously. (We will say more about that in the next chapter.) However, it may be necessary to let the kinds of prewriting we have been discussing generate a preliminary plan of some kind. On a project using notes and research information, some sort of juggling of note cards into a specific (but tentative) order may be needed; the nice thing about note cards is that you can shuffle them around, lay them out on a table or floor, rearrange them, delete the ones that do not fit the emerging pattern of the piece, and organize the ones that do into an order you can follow like an outline. Another alternative is to create an outline, which can be either a sketchy general plan or a carefully crafted blueprint. These forms of prewriting not only prepare a writer to get started on the draft, but they can also serve as a means of guiding the draft as it is being written. For that reason, we will look more carefully at these two forms of prewriting in the next chapter.

Holding off on the discussion of note-card posting and outlining also gives me an occasion to iterate (or reiterate) that composing is not performed in simple self-contained steps. Just as string-saving and prewriting often occur simultaneously, so do prewriting and drafting. A simple sentence written down when a thought arises can survive from random string-saving through intensive revising, can even be the instigation of the entire work. For that reason, although engaging in prewriting of some sort is important, planning the draft in such detail that the drafting is essentially transcribing rather than composing usually is not necessary—in fact, it may be impossible. The experienced wordsmith never begins drafting before she is ready; prewriting, of whatever amount or scope, is chiefly a way of getting ready for drafting. Often a writer will discover at some point in the prewriting that she has been drafting as well, simultaneously. At that point she is ready to begin the drafting in earnest.

4 DRAFTING

A writer who has been regularly engaged in string-saving and who has recently engaged in prewriting the work he hopes to write is in a better position to begin drafting than the writer who suddenly realizes a deadline is nearly due and who begins examining the call for manuscripts or the class assignment in hopes of some clues about how to start a draft. The draft is something that comes out of the writer, not out of the assignment or the call for manuscripts, and the writer who has not been working on the project in some form before attempting a draft is either bluffing, trusting blindly in sudden inspiration, or simply confused about the process of writing. One of the chief causes of frustration in writing, including writing blocks, is premature drafting, which forces the writer to discover, plan, and compose simultaneously, a difficult enough task for an accomplished wordsmith, a discouraging, sometimes devastating one for a novice. In writing, as in so many other things, the readiness is all.

The Advantages of Readiness

Readiness can help alleviate two common fears about drafting: the paltry draft fear, or fear of having nothing to say, and the dry well fear, or fear that "if we write what's in our heads, we will run out of words and ideas" (Warnock 309). To overcome the paltry draft fear we have to come to the drafting ready to lower standards and expectations, ready to accept the writing as incomplete, unpolished, uncertain; to overcome the dry well fear we have to believe that "writing can prime the pump instead of draining it" and that "the more the well is pumped, the greater the yield" (Warnock 309).

But readiness does not necessarily mean having a large block of time in which to complete the project in one sitting. Richard Reeves, the columnist, once went through a period in which he tried to complete long articles in a single composing session; however, he discovered that a reader could trace the flow of his energy in the articles, from his lively opening to his weary conclusions. An important part of drafting is recognizing that composing takes place over time—you can write separate portions on different occasions, allowing yourself to focus fully on one small task at a time, because you get a chance later on to revise the entire work. In the revising you can connect portions with logical transitions and arrange or rearrange sections to suit an overlying sense of structure. Depending on the project, such an approach uses the composing process to your advantage. If, on the other hand, you attempt single-sitting, first-and-final drafts, you are imposing on yourself severe handicaps to successful completion of the project. Thus, a cardinal rule of drafting is to allow yourself enough time, not only for initial drafting of portions, but also for the preliminary work and the revising; a corollary to that rule is to never expect to complete a writing project in a single sitting.

Discovery During Drafting

Some of the reasoning behind these rules have to do with the nature of drafting itself. We have discussed the element of discovery through writing earlier, but in truth discovery is not something that happens only prior to drafting—it also happens during drafting. All the elaborate plot outline of a short story cannot keep characters from revealing unexpected facets of their personalities once the writer is trying to capture them on the page; all the careful listing of pros and cons for an argument you want to make cannot prevent you from stumbling on an unlooked-for weakness or serendipitous item of support in the course of explaining your position; all the clustering of reminiscences gathered as a preliminary to drafting a nostalgic essay cannot stop fresh memories from surfacing as you write about those you already recalled; all the careful gathering of resources and assembling of quotes prior to writing a research paper cannot eliminate the recognition of the gaps in your information and understanding and the need for further research. The very act of drafting generates discovery; writing is never the mere recording of separately prepared thoughts. The experienced wordsmith knows and relies on this aspect of drafting; the inexperienced wordsmith sometimes gets thrown by it.

Consider, for example, the nature of a zero draft, introduced in chapter 3. A zero or discovery draft is a long way from the final draft, so much in need of revision that it barely counts as a rough draft. An experienced writer may launch into the writing of a zero draft without much concern for the direction it takes in order to use the draft as a means "to discover ideas that emerge at the ends of sentences, paragraphs, and papers" (Warnock 309). Perhaps the writing project is one where prewriting and planning of more structured kinds is less advantageous, such as writing a personal essay exploring feelings and memories. The zero draft is really a part of the prewriting rather than the drafting, because its function is chiefly to provide a text to work from in composing a rough draft. Even the much-admired essayist E. B. White claimed, "I always write a thing first and think about it afterward, which is not a bad procedure, because the easiest way to have consecutive thoughts is to start putting them down" (White 224–225).

The wordsmith writes a discovery draft willingly but tentatively, just to see what she has to work with; she knows she will better understand her point of view (or the nature of the story she has to tell or the argument that arises from the evidence she has gathered) once she has put something in writing. Annie Dillard, having written a discovery draft of an essay in her journal and having decided to work on developing it, took out some paragraphs immediately because they were

> the kind of absurdity you fall into when you write about anything, let alone yourself. You're so pleased and grateful to be writing at all, especially at the beginning, that you babble. Often you don't know where the work is going, so you can't tell what's irrelevant.

It doesn't hurt to babble in a first draft, so long as you have the
sense to cut out irrelevancies later. ("How" 17)

An inexperienced writer may produce a zero draft without recognizing it for what it is and attempt to treat it as if it were an advanced formal draft. Particularly in projects where writers launch
themselves out without much incubation and prewriting, the text
itself determines its own development far more than it would if
the writer had some sort of writing plan, no matter how sketchy.
Often in such cases the constraints on the composing cancel one
another out, so that uncertainty about the organization interferes
with development of ideas and examples and expression of language. The discovery draft often produces a text that the writer
can use to focus on structure later on or it can reveal problems of
development that suggest ways of adding detail and illustration in
a later draft. These are often the reasons an intended rough draft
becomes a zero draft, because the issues of organization and development had not been resolved before the drafting began.

The Shifting Concerns of Drafting Sessions

Organization and development are global concerns in a piece of
writing; sentence structure and precise vocabulary are local concerns. The global concern with structure usually needs to be addressed before the local concern of style, not the other way
around. In a draft it makes little sense to worry mightily over the
exact wording of a section that structurally does not fit in the text.
In the revision of an early draft (particularly a zero draft) many
paragraphs get jettisoned to create a more appropriately balanced
structure. It is easy to imagine the frustration of working on sentence-level problems in those paragraphs only to have to throw
them out because they really have nothing to do with the final
topic of the paper. Sometimes, when a draft has been well prepared for and rehearsed, structure and style are created smoothly,
simultaneously. More often, however, they have to be considered
separately; when they are, structure usually takes precedence
over style in the drafting and early revision stages.
     Wordsmiths who understand the need for the writing to go
through a process of discovery and change free themselves from the

burden of inappropriate expectations. For example, David Denby, film critic for *New York Magazine*, does not worry about careful crafting or choosing exactly the right sentences in the first draft. Instead, he says,

> because I know I'm going to do another draft, I try to get it down on paper in the right order and get it to say more or less what I want it to say and not be too fussy about specific wording. (Root 181)

When he comes to revise he does the work more willingly. He says,

> The second draft goes much more quickly and I find it very pleasurable. I find the first draft agony; the second draft I think is a lot of fun when you actually have something there to work with, to play with. It's at that point that your feelings of craftsmanship take over. . . . (Root 182)

Denby's experience is replicated by a host of other writers, all with their own variations of the process. They have had to evolve a process that works specifically for them, even if it would hamper the writing of another writer. More important, they have developed strategies for dealing with the roadblocks that often emerge in writing. Revising is an important part of those strategies, because the reliance on revising for content, style, and expression frees up their concentration for the development and discovery of ideas earlier in the process.

Thus far I have been insisting that the best approach to drafting is to come to it prepared to write and fully aware that it may take more than one session. By the same token, when you know you have to have another session, the best place to stop drafting is before you have run out of ideas. Try to stop when you still have something you want to add. Make a note of it or write a log entry about what you have to do next before you quit, but try to know what you will be doing at the next session. In other words, come to each drafting session prepared to write.

Experienced wordsmiths have noted that sitting in front of a word processor or typewriter or yellow legal pad, staring at the blankness and wondering for the first time what might fill it up, can lead to discouraging, unproductive sessions. You want to be able to get started as soon as possible at each session; coming prepared, even eager, to write is the best way to do it. Trust yourself that if you have something in mind, your subconscious will work on it for you in the interval between sessions and probably add to it, and when you do start drafting again, you will set the whole session in motion. Some wordsmiths have compared the process to pumping water from a well until it is low (never until it is dry) and then giving time for more water to seep in from the aquifer so that the well is full again the next time you need to use it. Several short composing sessions are often more productive than one long make-or-break session, because in the intervals between sessions, things happen to the ideas, to the language being rehearsed, almost despite the writer's intentions. By the same token, those composing sessions ought to be regular enough and frequent enough for you to maintain momentum on the project. Long layoffs between composing sessions on a single project interfere with the composing, because you lose track of where you were and where you hoped to go, and searching for the lost thread of your earlier efforts wastes time and energy and encourages you to defer composing.

Just as short intervals in between sessions are valuable for the productivity of the sessions, so an interval between drafting and revising is valuable to get some distance, some perspective on what you have written. Never write and submit anything in white heat. Your closeness to the composing will encourage you to stay loyal to every word, every punctuation mark; ideas, because fresh, will seem exactly right. Giving yourself some time between drafting and revising helps you to be more objective about your writing; you forget what you had intended to say and have to deal with what you really said—not always the same thing. This is another reason for giving yourself enough time for a project—coming back to a draft after an interval of letting it lie, even if it is only a day or two, will give freshness to the reading and more effectiveness to the revision.

For the actual drafting itself, knowing the kinds of strategies that other writers use is helpful, but there are probably as many ways to draft texts as there are writers. Some writers need to curl up in a favorite chair with a favorite pen and legal pad for the rough draft; others use a typewriter and plenty of paper, X-ing out deletions and typing over changes; still others need the bouncing cursor of the word processor. Some insist on silence, some want specific kinds of "white noise" in the background, some can write no matter where or when. I use a variety of approaches, depending on what I'm writing, but often I like room to walk around in between bursts of drafting. Hemingway wrote standing up. Others can only write lying down. Whatever the place or the circumstances or the approach you take, it is a good idea to have a specific writing place and a block of writing time, even if it is only an hour or even a half hour. These help you stop yourself from doing other things that distract you from your writing. To help even further, these should be inviolable blocks of time, when the phone is unplugged or the door shut. Even small blocks of time, in a series, can produce good work over time.

Ways of Drafting

So far as the actual drafting itself goes, that may vary with the project and the circumstances, but it probably ought to be consistent for the duration of the project and intended ahead of time. Following are some ways of drafting.

1. *Free-flow drafting* lets you start out from your string-saving and prewriting with at least a sense of where to begin and then lets your drafting follow the train of thought that the writing generates. This is an example of letting the text produced so far determine the text to be produced. In cases where the structure is fairly predictable (you have a thesis statement you will support with half a dozen arguments or you have a story to tell that is fairly simple) and where you have had plenty of time to incubate and rehearse, this can often produce a pretty usable draft. When I wrote short (three to four pages) essays for a local public radio station, I usually used this approach, because the length and the format were very familiar (I eventually wrote nearly 250 essays over eight years) and because I could use a casual style to talk about subjects on my mind. Most of them had been rehearsed in conversation or contemplation during walks to work or they grew out of things I had long mulled over in memory or recently reacted to strongly. My constant engagement with the essay series

kept me continuously preparing to write, so the things I wrote about in a free-flow style were things ready to be written about. When I became too constantly engaged in experiences that did not serve that form or allow that time for rehearsal and gestation, I had to give up writing for radio.

Free-flow drafting for a project based on research or critical analysis of other texts, as often is assigned in academic courses, ought to start after references have been collected, sources consulted, and notes reviewed. Considerable thought ought to go into the opening paragraph, so that the text that emerges in the drafting starts in a place that promises connections to major ideas later on. Launching yourself off into free-flowing drafting for a project that depends on information outside yourself is obviously riskier than doing it on a project that depends on personal experience, knowledge, and memory.

The danger with free-flow drafting is that you might start the draft without sufficient string-saving and prewriting, in which case you will produce a zero draft or you will get launched on the draft and then flounder because you really had nowhere to go with it beyond the initial opening. Wordsmiths of long standing have file cabinets filled with false starts—that's no disgrace; but defeat can be discouraging, and unless you are willing to risk it and willing to acknowledge and accept it (a good many failed student papers get submitted from a dogged unwillingness to throw out anything labored on), you would be better off trying one of the other approaches to drafting.

2. *Outlining* is a more traditional method and can be frustrating if you hope to follow it exactly and largely flesh it out with prose to make a paper. Tinkering with an outline can be part of the discovery process in prewriting, but often the drafting discovers new things that do not fit the outline. Instead, a rough outline can often be used as a general guide, a road map to where you are going and what you have to pass through to get there. For example, working on the armadillo assignment mentioned in chapter 2, one student generated a loose outline that looked like this:

> Name: "little armored thing" (Spanish)
> Originated: South America. Now from Rio Grande to Oklahoma to Louisiana.
> Food: Termites, scorpions, snakes

Armor: horny scales rather than hair. Fuse together to form
shields over front & back. Midregion form jointed
bands for flexibility. Protection from flesh-eaters.
Teeth: Order "Edentata," lack of enamel on teeth. Small,
piglike, lacking roots.
Feet: Toes clawed for digging.
Breeding: Polyembryony. 4 identical quadruplets—division
of single egg. 8–9 mo. gestation.
Species: 21–9-banded (Dasypus novemcinctus) only one in
U.S. Smallest—fairy (Chlamyphorous) mole-like 5 in.
(13 cm) Largest—giant (Priodontis) 5 ft. (150 cm)
Family: Dasypodiae 9 genera
Timid, nocturnal, bury themselves from pursuers

In drafting the piece, she would expand on each of these items in
order as she wrote, using the outline to determine sequence and
following the hints accompanying the categories to assure her of
covering what she felt were important points. The information in
the last line was really separate from the outline, and she would
attempt to use it wherever she could fit it in.

Another student gave herself a scantier road map:

Order—What it looks like/physical features/size—
What it eats
Where it lives
Mating habits
Its young
Ancestors
Kinds/best known
Folklore—literary connections
Life cycle

Because her outline is so sparse, she will essentially work on
each section as a unit, referring back to the source articles and
her notes, focusing only on the information needed for that section while she drafts. The outline is chiefly to remind her of the
order of information; the drafting itself will arise out of the notes
and sources.

One further road map: in this case the student has made an
outline of the structure of the draft she intends to write, then left

room to mention what subtopics within those headings she will need to address; to further organize them she put numbers in front of them to indicate the order she should follow and references to one of the three articles (A, B, or C) after them to remind her where to find the information when she needs it.

Armadillo
1. Where they are located
      Only 9-banded in U.S.
      So. America
2. Size/types
      p. C
      Species p. B
3. Body—
      "Make-up" 1. p. A 2. underside, tail p. B
      as protection   5. tongue   p. B
                         4. snout   p. C
                         3. teeth   p. C
      3A. What they eat Timid, nocturnal p. B
4. Breeding/Reproduction/Life Cycle
      p. B
      p. C unusual life cycle
5. Benefits
      p. C
      p. A eats termites & other insects
            incl. scorpions, also snakes
      p. B as food
6. Prehistory
      p. A
      p. B
7. Folklore p. A
8. Conclusion

To someone unfamiliar with the three articles this outline only gives a rough order of general topics and provides no useful information about the subject, but it serves the writer herself very well because it categorizes and locates information and frees her up to deal with one element of this material at a time rather than making her hold it all in her head and juggle everything simultaneously.

An outline serves as an aid to drafting if you work on the outline before drafting and expect to change it as you write the draft. The outline needs to be flexible and fluid, changing and growing with your awareness of your text. It also helps you get some sense of proportion about the draft and alerts you when your train of thought has gotten derailed. When made after completing a draft, an outline is a good way of finding out what you have said; numbering the paragraphs and listing their main contents in an outline can help you understand the flow of your ideas and the relative proportion of the elements. In any event, the outline has to be a flexible aid to drafting, not a rigid dictator of it.

3. *Note-card posting* is particularly useful for papers based on research, although it can also help any piece of writing in which there are pieces of prewriting that indicate sections of the proposed draft. John McPhee's method with notes is well known. According to William Howarth, McPhee takes a multitude of notes for whatever project he is working on and, when he feels he has enough, he "transcribes the notebooks, typing entries in order, occasionally adding other details or current thoughts as he goes" (McPhee xiv). He then photocopies that typescript and puts the original into a binder he can read through, at first perhaps making new notes and typing them up to add to the binder, then taking notes on patterns and possible structures. Once he has decided on the approach he will take to the subject, he codes the notes according to their topics and labels a series of index cards, which he sorts, arranges, and attaches to a bulletin board. In a sense he is making the outline of the article or book; the index cards give him great flexibility in rearranging the structure.

Then he cuts up the photocopied set of notes and arranges the pieces by putting them in folders labeled in accordance with the index cards. He files the folders and then works on the writing by tackling the topic on each index card in order and consulting the corresponding file folder. "A large steel dart on the bulletin board marks his progress. He stabs the dart under an index card, opens a folder, further sorts scraps and ribbons until this segment also has a logical structure" (McPhee xv). It is an elaborate system for someone writing dense, complicated works, but it helps him break up the drafting into manageable sections and it helps him prepare for the drafting. As he has said, when the note cards are posted, "you're liberated now; there's nothing between you and the blank page" (Schuster). Working section by section he will produce multiple drafts to piece together as the work progresses. "You don't want something that's too finished or polished too early in the game," he says. "Learn to live with the rough drafts or else you'll produce no draft at all" (Schuster). People working on less ambitious projects can use the same system in a simpler way, by arranging note cards to produce a working outline—tacking them to a bulletin board, lining them up on a table, laying them out on the floor—and giving themselves a visual sense of the arrangement of the parts. At the same time it also almost automatically helps arrange the drafting into more manageable sections.

4. *Segmented composing* is working on the project in sections, not necessarily in so systematic a way as McPhee's approach through note-card posting. As mentioned earlier, Richard Reeves's documentary film scripts are written a scene at a time, not necessarily in the order in which they appear in the final screenplay. Many writing projects can be broken into sections and the sections worked on out of sequence. For example, in the social sciences, reports on research often begin with a review of previous research followed by a section describing a specific research project, a section describing results of that research, and a section drawing conclusions or discussing the implications of the results. Although there is a logical progression of the parts, the actual composition of each part need not follow the sequence of the final text. John Jerome offers another example of segmented composing in his book *The Writing Trade*, where he describes how he established several computer files for a long magazine article on New Hampshire, typed his notes once on the word processor, and then moved or copied them into the appropriate files electronically. He explains:

> Those notes will be very rough; the job then will be to expand and develop the ideas in them, to put them into effective sentences, to try to make them fit the flow of the piece. When it comes time to write the text proper, I'll be pulling paragraphs out of the files and dropping them into place if I get stuck—if I'm having trouble advancing the text or figuring out where to go with it next—I can always go to any of the five files and start sharpening the paragraphs there, before they're tossed into the text. That process usually generates enough new thoughts to get me going again on the piece itself.
>
> The power of this working method—for me—is that it lets me work as if the writing of the piece is just a case of cutting and

pasting. It breaks into manageable pieces the otherwise daunting job of putting together a long, organized piece. When I lose headway in one place, I can always find someplace else to put my time until the next step makes itself clear. As a working method it is very self-protective, saving me from ever having to face a blank sheet of paper. (51–52)

In later stages of revision he can work on the connections between segments, the decisions about sequence, the elimination of repetition, the establishment of transitions, the introductory material for the piece he has actually written, and the concluding material appropriate for the segments that precede it.

5. *Incremental composing* is more of a start-and-stop method of drafting that may begin from a point where the writer feels confident enough to start drafting but uncertain about direction and expecting the drafting itself to generate discoveries necessary for the composing to continue. One good example of incremental composing comes from Connie Leas, a technical writer who described her composing process for writing an instruction manual for a computer program: "My system would consist of: get an idea of the big picture, make an outline, then learn-write-revise-learn-write-revise until it's done" (Leas). Having gathered together a great deal of information and working from ever-changing outlines ("The more I'd learn about it the more I'd keep changing the outline") she would work on sections of the program until she discovered information she did not understand, then either work through to an understanding or consult others who were more proficient with the program.

> You need to have an idea of the big picture but you can't begin to know all the details so what you do—what I do—is, just start. In the process I begin to learn.... You're learning about the thing you're writing about usually while you're writing about it. The writing of something will make you realize that there're pieces of it you don't get.

The work moves forward incrementally, growing with the writer's knowledge through the drafting itself.

6. *Page guides* are used by some writers who have a sense of how long a piece will run to indicate what they ought to be writing about when they reach certain sections of the paper. *De-*

troit Free Press columnist Jim Fitzgerald will write along the margin of a sheet of paper the relative positions of the topics he intends to address in his column-in-progress; he places the sheet on the desk beside his word processor and consults it as he types his first draft, adding or deleting items on the sheet as new or different ideas arise in the drafting. Richard Reeves has sometimes used the same approach on columns he has had to draft on legal pads, composing on a plane or in a hotel room. The notes in the margin remind him of the relative location of different items in the draft; because he knows from experience how the length of the longhand draft compares with a typed draft, he knows about where he needs to be making each of his points and starting to prepare for his conclusion. Like an outline or an arrangement of notes, the page guide is simply a way of keeping yourself on track and preventing the text itself from taking over the composing process.

7. *Channeled composing* is, in one sense, not unlike free-flow drafting, because both work their way through the text by letting the composing itself influence the direction of the text; but in another sense, it is the exact opposite, because it is carried out by careful intense drafting that includes intensive revising. The drafting does not flow freely but rather is a constant endeavor to channel the flow of the text. Each sentence is worked on carefully before moving to the next, and then when the next is completed, the two together have to be examined before moving on to a third. Particularly when the ideas in a text have been thoroughly rehearsed (in thought or in prewriting activities) this approach to drafting can be effective in carefully constructing the text. Annie Dillard writes,

> The reason to perfect a piece of prose as it progresses—to secure each sentence before building on it—is that original writing fashions a form. It grows cell to cell, bole to bough to twig to leaf; any careful word may suggest a route, may begin a strand of metaphor or event out of which much, or all, will develop. Perfecting the work inch by inch, writing from the first word toward the last, displays the courage and fear this method induces. (*Writing* 15)

The free-flow approach assumes you can always go back to it and revise; the investment is not so great you feel you have to protect it at any cost. The channeled approach gambles that you can get through this in one controlled draft, and sometimes the gamble pays off. Often, however, especially for inexperienced writers, it does not. As Annie Dillard *also* observes,

> The reason not to perfect a work as it progresses is that, concomitantly, original work fashions a form the true shape of which it discovers only as it proceeds, so the early strokes are useless, however fine their sheen. Only when a paragraph's role in the context of the whole work is clear can the envisioning writer direct its complexity of detail to strengthen the work's ends. (*Writing* 16)

In practice, then, the first six approaches are safer strategies.

Choosing Among Drafting Strategies

These drafting strategies are not mutually exclusive; all can be used in combination with one another. The strategy you use may be the one that seems to work the best for you or, more likely, the one that seems to work the best for the writing you have to do. Personal narratives, for example, are often easier to draft in a free-flowing style than a library research project or a formal report, because they are essentially stories about what happened, and the major focus of the draft is chiefly getting the details in the proper order with the appropriate balance between them; the other two types of projects involve collecting data from other sources, analyzing and rearranging it, and figuring out a way of presenting it to a reader that clarifies the relationships among the bits of information. Such a project may call for more structured approaches to drafting. Experienced wordsmiths know that they can draw on a range of writing strategies as the need arises and circumstances invite. Elaine Maimon, an academic writer, says,

> I find that my writing practices vary within a single project and, more particularly, from project to project. Sometimes I start writing a draft without a specific plan in mind. More often, I have a shopping list of points I wish to cover or images I want to invoke. Once in a while, I make an outline from rough notes. I deem myself to be an experienced writer because I have learned flexibility and the capacity for systematic variability. (142–143)

The number of sessions that a writing project demands also depends on the nature of the writing project. Obviously it is better to plan for more sessions rather than for less, particularly if you are working toward a deadline. Discovering that you do not need all the sessions you had scheduled yourself—because the work is going better than you anticipated—is preferable to discovering that you will need many more sessions than you predicted—because the work is not going well. In addition, the number of sessions may depend on how much string-saving and preliminary work has already been done, how familiar you are with the material you are writing about, how accustomed to the format you intend to be writing in—it may depend, that is, on how ready you are to start drafting.

An Example of Drafting: The Hitchhiker Essay

The piece that I had begun to work on about the hitchhiker, introduced earlier, proved to be a challenging little essay, in part because of the limits imposed on it by the place I hoped to submit it. I needed to tell the story, create her character and my conflict, give a sense of place, and keep it all within 450 words. The journal had recorded my initial meeting with her and my strong reaction; the discovery draft had revealed to me certain things I wanted to get across—her personality, my timidity as opposed to her adventurousness, the likelihood that this encounter prompted me to do my first solo camping trip. But the discovery draft was not acceptable as a rough draft of the essay—it didn't create character as much as I wanted, it explained too much and showed too little, it didn't get across the contrast between us and my eventually adapting her attitude the way I now knew I wanted. So I started over from scratch with a new draft, that ended up being the draft I would revise through to publication (see Figure 4-1). In this draft I tried to show everything through the conversation and then toward the end get around to the idea of my initial reaction to her and my eventual venturing out on my own. Because this piece is so short it was easy to work through a draft in a single sitting. The discovery draft was pretty much free-flow composing;

1

~~There was something anachronistic about the red-headed young hitchhiker, something hippylike and out of the Sixties.~~ The red-headed young hitchhiker, ~~casually wearing a~~ *dressed in* tee-shirt and jeans, *a duffle bag at her feet,* had the flaky serenity of a flower child. She was cheerful and chatty from the moment I picked her up, *on I-75* South of Flint. When we passed the exit ~~on I-75~~ for Oakland University, I told her a friend of mine from college, whom I hadn't seen for thirteen years, was teaching there. She said I ought to find out when his classes met and just go sit in one. "It would really freak him out," she laughed.

I laughed with her, as much at her pleasure at imagining Football's response as at the thought of surprising him. She was an interesting, open person, a pleasant surprise for someone who had expected to be traveling alone. *I was on my way to Grosse Pointe to stay overnight with friends but I felt guilty about the stack of ungraded papers* ~~I had been bound for Grosse Pointe, feeling odd about staying overnight with friends and leaving my schoolwork behind; much as I~~ I'd left behind in my apartment, ~~driving like someone late for an appointment, when~~ and I continually caught myself driving with the grim determination of someone late for a business meeting. It was dawning on me that I seldom left home for any reason that wasn't ~~motivated~~ *somehow connected* with my teaching.

My hitchhiker had had different reasons for not traveling as much as she'd like. "Usually I'm living with some dude and can't really have a vacation." The irony ~~of that~~ was that one of them now was wandering around all over the Western United States while she was still in Michigan, working part-time as a musician. But she took disappointment lightly, accepted it with only a few words of regret. "A friend was going to travel with me this weekend but his wife wouldn't let him. ~~What a bummer."~~ *It's really a* bummer." I nodded sympathetically.

FIGURE 4-1. Rough Draft

2

She was on her way to Canada for the weekend. ~~I asked~~ but when I asked her ~~where~~ what city, she didn't have a destination in mind. I said I'd let her off near the tunnel where she could catch a ride or maybe walk across.

"Is there a toll? Do you think it's more than $2.35?"

"I don't even know if you can walk across. Why did you say '$2.35'?"

"Because that's all I have with me."

"How can you afford to go to Canada for a weekend on $2.35?"
~~"You're going to Canada for the weekend on $2.35?" The Dutch uncle in me was struggling to reach the surface. I restrained him and~~

"Oh, I'll probably get a gig in Windsor tonight playing piano." She shrugged. "Something will turn up."

We were pretty near the Ren Cen. She said that it freaked her out. I dropped her near the tunnel to Canada, neither of us certain that she could cross. ~~She slung~~ Her duffle bag over her shoulder, her thongs slapping on the pavement, she strode off one way, to unplanned adventure and I drove off the other ~~way.~~ to my safe haven in Grosse Pointe.

I wanted to shake my head and write her off as ~~a~~ either pleasantly dizzy ~~flower child and~~ or unbelievably ingenuous. But something in me was challenged. I wondered why I at age 36 had to wait and worry about finances and attention to unrewarding responsibilities while she at 22 or so could brave the world unprepared on $2.35. Perhaps she was foolhardy but was I so afraid of life that I couldn't reach out for it without safety measures all around me?

Two weeks later ~~I was~~ camp(ed)ing alone on the Leelanau Peninsula, all my obligations left behind me for a weekend. I fell asleep to the sound of Lake Michigan and strolled beaches and woods like a vagabond. I even climbed Sleeping Bear Dunes. They really freaked me out.

FIGURE 4-1. (continued)

this draft is more controlled, sort of semi-channeled composing— a general sense of structure was mapped in my head, and I took some pains to direct the drafting to cover the ground I now realized I wanted to cover.

Drafting and Other Elements of Composing

At least one more thing needs to be said about drafting, and it relates back to the constant subtext of this book—that we are not talking about discreet, distinct stages of writing in each chapter but rather about certain moments of concentration on various strategies for composing. Throughout the drafting you may find yourself planning and preparing, on the one hand, and revising, on the other. After all, your plans are not set in concrete and your revisions do not have to—cannot—wait until the drafting is done. That being the case, you may consider a draft completed when you feel you have to focus on it in a different way than you have been so far, when you feel instead that you ought to go back over the whole of it and make it come together better (revising), or when you feel you ought to work on its appearance and eliminate stumbling blocks to a comfortable reading of it (editing or proofreading).

This may not require a complete draft, however. In many academic papers, for example, the ideas you need to present in the final section of the paper or the conclusion depend so much on the clarity and logic of the evidence you have presented that you simply *cannot* write the conclusion until you have revised the central section first. By the same token, writing the beginning of the paper is often difficult until the rest of the paper is substantially finished, because the beginning section of a paper introduces the reader to the ideas that make up the rest of the paper. Laboring on the introduction can be frustrating because you may not know enough about the content you are trying to introduce and will not until you have discovered or learned more by trying to write about it. Conclusions are easier to write—they conclude the paper you have already written. Introductions are harder—if written first, they introduce the paper you hope to write, the one that may have to change the most as drafting opens new doors. (Once, clearing out my filing cabinet of fifteen years worth of old drafts, I discovered that most of my energy in revising went into the first half of my papers.) Sometimes it is better to launch yourself into the center of your paper first, work it through, then write your conclusion, and finally write your introduction. When that is the case, clearly a draft can be considered only a substantial section of the paper, not a complete version of the entire work.

Thoreau once observed in his journal that, in a writer's first attempt to write on a subject, "he produces scarcely more than a frame and groundwork" because "each clear thought that he attains to draws in its train many divided thoughts or perceptions." For this reason,

> the writer has much to do even to create a theme for himself. Most that is first written on any subject is a mere groping after it, mere rubble-stone and foundation. It is only when many observations of different periods have been brought together that he begins to grasp his subject and can make one pertinent and just observation. (11:438–439)

The prudent wordsmith, then, approaches drafting as an opportunity to discover the foundation she will build on, takes a flexible position concerning the progress of the work at hand, and does not expect to work on the finishing touches of the edifice until she is certain that what she is building is solid enough outside to support the interior walls that demand more painstaking work.

5 REVISING

Revising, like composing itself, is most successful when the writer has a clear, practical model of it to direct him. When the model is inaccurate or irrelevant, successful revising is impossible. Often, particularly among novice writers, revising is confused with transcription or editing or proofreading, and subsequently such writers tend to do those tasks instead of actually revising. By *transcription* I simply mean copying the text over neatly; *editing* means going through a text carefully, line by line, to examine the sentence structure, the grammar and usage, the clarity and accuracy—the last time the writer wrestles chiefly with expression of ideas; *proofreading* is the review of the final copy to make certain that it contains no errors in text preparation, misspellings, typos, misnumberings, inconsistent documentation, and the like. All three of these tasks are usually necessary to complete a writing project by preparing a *presentation text* of the work (something we will consider in the next chapter), but they are also all tasks that, by and large, can be performed by someone other than the writer. Publications routinely employ typists and typesetters, editors, and proofreaders expressly for these purposes, although they are tasks any writer has to make best efforts at completing successfully before submitting final copy. However, transcription, editing, and proofreading are almost wholly about correction, but revising is about rethinking and potentially making substantial changes in structure or sense. It is about moving the text from a point where something that has been expressed is ready to be reexamined and perhaps expressed in a different way, where an initial draft of the whole work (or significant sections) has reached a point where it is possible to review, reconsider, or perhaps replace and reformulate it.

The Differences Between Drafting and Revising

Revising does not mean starting from scratch all over again. Throwing out everything you have done and beginning anew produces a first (or rough or zero) draft, not a revision. The revision retains what is working in the earlier draft and eliminates and replaces what is not. The ability to revise—and the willingness as well—is central to becoming an accomplished wordsmith. Annie Dillard in *The Writing Life* makes the comparison of a writer facing a draft that is not working with a builder examining a house that is not being constructed the way it should (4). The builder hopes that, if anything has to be removed, it will be a decorative wall, not a bearing wall holding up the whole structure; but even if it is a bearing wall that has to go and the whole edifice has to be torn down to the foundation, the builder has to be willing to do it. So too must the wordsmith treat none of the writing as indispensable, preservable at any cost; in the end it is the soundness of the edifice that matters, not the ease or speed of its construction. Much that is weak in the final draft of a piece of writing comes from the reluctance of the writer to remove it or the inability of the writer to recognize that it needs removing.

For that reason the advice in chapter 4 about letting the text sit for a while before attempting revision is an important one. (Try reading a paper you wrote a year or two ago and you'll see what I mean.) Time off gives you the distance you need to see your work from the perspective of someone else; some of the prose will surprise you, because you won't recall having written it. That gives you the chance to be objective about it, less committed to every aspect of the work you have completed. You will more eas-

ily see the need for revision if you yourself have difficulty following your argument or understanding an allusion or example or
untangling the syntax of a sentence. The time away from the writing does not allow your mind to cover for your confusion the way
it does when the reading immediately follows the writing. Equally
important, even as the time off helps you identify weaknesses, it
also makes it possible for you to identify strengths you might otherwise overlook or discard inadvertently. You have a better sense
of what is working and what is not. Depending on the complexity
of the project, in most early drafts not everything is working
equally well.

Some writers have years to work on projects, and some of
them never actually get around to completing them—there is no
pressure to do so. Student writers, by contrast, have lots of pressure on them to finish their writing tasks hurriedly. Consequently,
they tend to opt for first-and-final drafts, revising while drafting
rather than stepping back from the draft. The result often is work
that simply is not as good as it could be (which actually can be
more disappointing than work that is not as good as the teacher
wanted it to be). But even in the rushed climate of college, a little
planning can give the writer a little time off to get away from the
draft, if only overnight or for a few hours. You can complete
the paper before you go to bed, then sleep on it and revise it in
the morning. Often your subconscious continues working on the
paper and the revision comes more easily. Or you can complete
the paper in the morning and give yourself until evening before
you revise it. Any gap between drafting and revising works to
your advantage. Ideally, you ought to shoot for an interval of a
few days or a week, and even confer with the teacher or other
students about a particularly difficult work-in-progress; but if the
reality of the school environment prevents this, even a little time
off can help.

I do not mean to suggest that drafting and revising are totally separate tasks—drafting involves constant revision, revision
often demands extensive new drafting—but I would encourage
most writers to plan specifically for revision in the time they allot
to their writing. When revision is performed as a new action after
you have more or less completed a draft, instead of as a subprocess of drafting itself, the revising task changes. You finally

get a chance to work on the piece as a whole rather than as an emerging portion.

Approaches to Revision

To begin with, give yourself some time in between drafting and revising, as little as a couple of hours, as much as several days—whatever it takes to get some distance from it and let the heat of creating cool. If you can work from clean copy, so much the better. It may vary for the individual writer, but generally an early draft with all its changes, strikeovers, deletions, and inserts can be difficult to envision as a total work; the labor of following its circuitous trail without getting sidetracked by dead ends can be an act of labyrinthine concentration that diverts attention from the entire design. The reason so many wordsmiths have converted to word processing, either entirely or in concert with manuscript or typescript, is simply that it makes the scribal portion of composing less laborious and painful and produces clean, readable copy so easily. The advantage of having a printed text to work on lies in the opportunity to see it fresh, as another writer might encounter it. Some writers revise directly on the video display terminal, some only by hand on hard copy, some both ways; I recommend working on hard copy at least once during revising—the contrast with the way the text looks on the screen is often revealing—and always before the final printing of presentation text.

One common way to revise is simply to begin at the first sentence of the draft or of the section that would come earliest and to read it carefully with a colored pen in hand (so that changes stand out against the black typeface of the hard copy), making changes as you go along. Particularly with a late or reasonably advanced draft, this method is likely to work well; it is especially useful as a strategy to edit rather than revise. But it is a problematical approach with an earlier draft, because it focuses attention on the text only at the sentence or paragraph level rather than on the whole work. Certainly at some point a writer has to attend to the ways the sentences go together, one after another, but there are more systematic strategies to choose from that engage the writer with the subject, format, and occasion for writing.

Assess What You Have Accomplished So Far

To begin with, you need some way of assessing whether your current draft achieves what you hoped it would. Rather than turn to the draft itself, it is often useful to step back from the draft and do some prewriting about the revision. Thoreau suggests such an approach when he writes in his journal:

> I find that I can criticize my composition best when I stand at a little distance from it,—when I do not see it, for instance. I make a little chapter of contents which enables me to recall it page by page to my mind, and judge it more impartially when my manuscript is out of the way. (6:190)

Without looking at the text itself, he attempts to think it through again, and the mental manipulation of the contents makes him think about structure and content without being inhibited by the actual draft.

Outline the Draft

One variation of this might be to actually make up a rough outline of the contents by going systematically through the text, forcing yourself to struggle with the ways the parts relate to one another. Annie Dillard writes, "If you are used to analyzing texts, you will be able to formulate a clear statement of what your draft turned out to be about. Then you make a list of what you've already written, paragraph by paragraph, and see what doesn't fit and cut it out. . . ." ("How" 17). As an example of how this might work in practice, consider the following drafts of a student paper.

FIRST DRAFT

How I Gained Self-Confidence
Through Waterskiing

    When I was about twelve years old I began to get this complex   1
that I was no good at anything. I had absolutely no self-confidence.
My little brother is one of those people that is good at almost any-

thing that he does. He is especially good in sports, which is where my complex came from. Ever since he was about ten, he has been able to beat me in almost anything. If he would play any sport—tennis, racquetball, ping-pong, badminton, or any other sport—he would beat me. I was always trying to find things that I was better in than he was. I never could find anything until I found that I had a real talent in waterskiing. It was from my first waterskiing tournament that I lost that lack of self-confidence.

2   It was the summer of 1979. My family and I were spending the summer up north at our cabin. I had wanted to enter a water-ski tournament for quite a while, but it wasn't until the summer of '79 that I seriously started to think about it. A friend of mine told me about the tournament about three weeks before it was to take place. So, now I had no excuse not to go, except for three obstacles I would have to overcome. They were first, I had to overcome my nervousness and trying to talk myself out of going. Second, I had to get the O.K. from my parents. And third, I had to get the day off. Now that wasn't going to be an easy task, since the place I was working was a canoe livery and our heaviest business was on the weekends, and the tournament was on a Sunday.

3   The first problem of trying to talk myself out of going wasn't too hard to overcome, because I really wanted to go ski in the tournament. I did, however, try to talk myself out of going a few times. But they were all unsuccessful because of my desire to go.

4   The second barrier wasn't so easy. Since I only had my license for a couple months my parents weren't very confident in my driving. They didn't want me to make a three hour drive to Grand Rapids by myself. After that I thought all had failed. Then, later that night a friend from home called to see if he could come up and visit some time, and by coincidence he was free the weekend of the tournament. So that was great, I had someone to ride with me. My parents didn't think it was so great though, but after some persuasion they said that I could go.

5   Then came the worst problem of the three. It was the one that I feared the most. In fact, I almost talked myself out of going because I was so scared to ask my boss for a Sunday off. I thought it would be no for sure, and it wouldn't be worth wasting my time or his. I went and asked him two weeks in advance.

Although he wasn't happy, when he found out why I wanted the day off he said go right ahead. I just about fainted when I heard him say yes, because it was such a surprise. I hit cloud nine when he answered me.

When I went home my parents were as shocked as I was   6
and started to reconsider, but I told them that they were backing out of their end of the deal. So they said I could go.

I began to practice every day before I would go to work.   7
And if it was still light out when I came from work, we would go out for a few runs. When I had bad runs I would get discouraged, and try to talk myself out of going because I just knew that I would get beat.

As the tournament got closer I got more nervous. I started   8
to try to talk myself out of it more and more. I began to make up excuses for not going. Excuses like, it's a long way to drive just to go skiing. I'll have to get up really early, I would save everyone at work a lot of problems if I didn't go, and so on. I told myself that I've come this far I'm not going to turn back now. That was the only thing that kept me from not going.

The day before the tournament finally came. I came home   9
from work just dead on my feet. I had planned on going to bed early, considering that I had to get up at five o'clock in the morning to leave for the tournament. To my misfortune some other friends of mine from home decided to come up and surprise me. Not knowing what I was doing the next day, they asked me to go see a movie with them. I got home at about eleven thirty and again I started to talk myself into not going because I would be so tired that I wouldn't be able to ski well at all. Again I overcame my anxiety.

We got up at five o'clock and took off. When we were about   10
five miles away from home I remembered that I didn't fill the car up with gas. When I looked at the gauge I only had a quarter of a tank. We went back and siphoned gas out of my friend's car. It gave us half a tank, and we left in hopes of finding an open gas station. Luckily as we were passing through a small town at six o'clock, a gas station was just opening. So my worries were all over.

11   We got to the tournament site without any further problems. Except, I was so nervous I could hardly talk. I kept picturing myself falling just as I was getting up. This was typical of how I thought then. I always pictured myself doing the worst possible thing.

12   I got positioned about tenth out of thirty. As I watched the other skiers go out and make mistakes I became a little more calm. When my turn came I was so nervous I wasn't able to speak. My concentration was at a peak. When I got done I was in first place. I couldn't hardly believe it. I watched the others as they came closer and closer to my score. Nobody reached it though. I had won my first tournament.

13   I was finally really good at something. Better than everyone else. Although I didn't go down to the tournament to prove myself, I had. I came home with the first place trophy to the surprise of many.

14   This incident was one of the most important parts of developing my self-confidence. This one in particular because it was the first, but two other tournaments that summer and a couple last summer have helped me gain amounts of confidence in myself. I found that with this boost of confidence I'm doing better in everything that I do. I'm doing better in school. I even give my little brother a hard time in the games that we play. It was because of this first ski tournament that I've gained confidence in myself.

By numbering the paragraphs and listing their contents in order the writer sees the following pattern in the paper:

1. General introduction of problem: Competition with brother, self-doubt; specific introduction to tournament
2. Introduction to tournament decision; introduction to three obstacles
3. Obstacle 1: Nervousness and self-doubt
4. Obstacle 2: Parents
5. Obstacle 3: Day off from work
6. Obstacle 2 again: Parents
7. Practice; Obstacle 1 again: Nervousness
8. Obstacle 1 again: Nervousness

9. Obstacle 4: Late night with friends
10. Travel to tournament; Obstacle 5: Gasoline
11. Arrival at tournament; Obstacle 1: Nervousness
12. Competition in tournament: Early skiers, my runs, later skiers, victory
13. Victory and what it meant to me
14. Conclusion: Victory and what it meant to me; competition with brother, self-confidence

The first draft is essentially stream of consciousness, a form of free-flow composing. The author is following the chronology of events, from the earlier lack of self-confidence and the initial decision to enter a waterskiing tournament through competition and victory in the tournament and the subsequent gaining of self-confidence. Because he starts the paper so far back in time, he finds himself considering the minor problems of preparing to attend the tournament rather than the actual competition. The sentences come out as they occur to him, and he repeats words, phrases, and ideas a great deal, because he hasn't discovered the best way to express his ideas. The first paragraph and the last paragraph are connected by the references to competition with his brother and the change from self-doubt to self-confidence, but the twelve paragraphs in between don't really focus on the achieving of self-confidence. In fourteen paragraphs only one, the twelfth, is really about the tournament.

Looked at in this way the author can recognize the balance between the parts in the structure he has produced and discover that although his intention might have been to write a paper recounting how he gained self-confidence his actual accomplishment has been a draft recounting how he overcame obstacles to get to his first waterskiing tournament. Before he does anything much with individual sentences, he has to decide what the structure of the paper is to be: does he want to change this to a paper on how he got to the tournament? does he want to keep the problems of getting there and expand the tournament section to be most important, doubling or tripling the length of the paper? does he want to focus on the tournament and jettison the obstacles to getting there?

Compare the first draft with the second. Here the student writer condenses seven paragraphs into one, abbreviates one paragraph of irrelevant travel details into a single sentence, and expands that single paragraph on the tournament into six paragraphs of description of the competition. It is now a paper about how he gained self-confidence through waterskiing.

SECOND DRAFT

How I Gained Self-Confidence Through Waterskiing

1   When I was about twelve years old I began to get this complex that I was no good at anything. I had absolutely no self-confidence. My little brother is one of those people that is good at almost anything that he does. He is especially good in sports, which is where my complex came from. Ever since he was about ten, he has been able to beat me in almost anything. If we would play any sport—tennis, racquetball, ping-pong, badminton, or any other sport—he would beat me. I was always trying to find things that I was better in than he was. I never could find anything until I found that I had a real talent in waterskiing. It was from my first waterskiing tournament that I lost that lack of self-confidence.

2   I had always wanted to enter a waterski tournament, but had never seriously considered it until the summer of 1979. A friend told me of a waterski tournament, and said that I should enter it. The tournament was about three weeks away, so I had no reason for not going. Except in the past I had had this problem of talking myself out of things like this. This time I wasn't going to let that happen, although I came close a couple of times. Also, my parents weren't going to be too keen on the idea of me driving three hours to Grand Rapids by myself, since I only had my license for a couple of months. Luckily a friend decided to go with me. So after a little persuasion, my parents decided to let me go. One last problem I was going to have to face was, I was going to have to get the day off. I thought for sure that I wouldn't be able to, but much to my surprise, when my boss heard what I wanted the day off for he said it would be no problem. I began to practice as hard as I could. Many times I became discouraged,

and would start cutting myself down, saying I would get beat, and it was stupid of me to even go. This was typical of the way I thought back then. Because of the way I was thinking I started to make excuses for not going. Excuses like, I'll have to get up really early, it is a long way to drive just to go skiing, and things like that. When I would catch myself thinking like this I would try to stop, and start thinking positive. It must have worked because I never successfully talked myself out of going.

Tournament day finally came and with great amounts of difficulty and anxiety, we made it down to the tournament on time to get registered.   3

I was picked to be tenth out of about thirty skiers. As I watched the first nine skiers go out and make mistakes I began to calm down a bit. As the first person went I thought that he must be one of the worst, and everyone was going to beat him. As the other skiers went I saw that it wasn't that the first skier was all that bad, because all the skiers were like that, it was just I had higher standards. I began to believe that I could do good in this tournament if I didn't make any serious mistakes. It was that thought of making a mistake that was making me nervous now.   4

As the boat pulled me out of the water I had a feeling of confidence like I had never had before. My concentration was higher than it ever was before. As I pulled across the wake and through the entrance gates, I knew it was going to be a good run. I can usually bet that if I don't get through the gates good then it will be a bad run, and if I get through them good then it will be a good run. Compared to my practice runs, I made it through the entrance gate perfectly. At this point I knew that if I could just make it around the first buoy I would be alright. I always seemed to have problems on the first buoy in practice. Once around the first buoy, the others came with great ease. I was relaxed as I went through the course. I had never been so relaxed before. Once I was through all six buoys I was shocked. It had never been so easy. It was almost too easy.   5

As the boat turned around to come back through, I was thinking that the speed the boat would be speeding up to was a speed that I never had made it through at before.   6

7   As I pulled through the entrance gates I almost fell. I began thinking, oh no it's going to be a bad run. Once around the first buoy everything was under control. Now I had five more to go. I began to ask myself if I could do it and set a personal record. As I rounded each buoy I was amazed at how easy they came compared to practice. It wasn't easy, but I was smooth and under control. I finally made it around the sixth buoy. I was in shock. I had set a personal record, if nothing else.

8   As the boat was turning around to pull me through again I began to see what a little confidence could do. As I came toward the course I decided to go for it and try to shatter my old record. It turned out that I fell going around the first buoy. It didn't really matter though. I had done better than I thought I would ever do. Also I was eleven buoys ahead of the second place person. I did realize, however, that twenty people still had to make runs. I still had confidence that my score would hold up.

9   As I watched the other skiers go, I realized they weren't any different than the first bunch of skiers. Although a couple skiers came close to my score, none of them beat it. I had done better than I ever expected to do both in the score that I received and in my placing. I had outscored the closest person by four full buoys, and that is quite a bit.

10   I was finally really good at something. Better than everyone else. Although I didn't go down to the tournament to prove myself, I had. I came home with the first place trophy to the surprise of many.

11   This incident was one of the most important parts of developing my self-confidence. This one in particular because it was the first, but two other tournaments that summer and a couple last summer have helped me gain amounts of confidence in myself. I found that with this boost of confidence I'm doing better in everything that I do. I'm doing better in school. I even give my little brother a hard time in the games that we play. It was because of this first ski tournament that I've gained confidence in myself.

A number of points need to be made about this revision. First, we need to notice the structure that emerges in the second draft.

1. General introduction of problem: Competition with brother, self-doubt; specific introduction to tournament
2. Introduction to tournament decision; introduction to three obstacles: Nervousness and self-doubt, parents, day off; practice and nervousness
3. Travel to and arrival at tournament
4. Early competitors
5. My first run: Part 1
6. Turning around for the 2nd part of my first run
7. My first run: Part 2
8. My second run and final score
9. Later competitors; victory
10. Victory and what it meant to me
11. Conclusion: Victory and what it meant to me; competition with brother, self-confidence

Clearly this is now a paper focused on the waterskiing tournament. The first draft turned out to be essentially a zero draft; the second is a rough draft of the paper that will eventually emerge from the assignment. Although he might have written the rough draft without having done the zero draft if he had done a sufficient amount of prewriting and planning, all the evidence of the zero draft suggests that the paper was done without planning and entirely in a single sitting. (That's why the tournament itself is described so quickly—the writer has spent two pages getting to the tournament and proportionately should spend about five more describing the competition; instead he hopes to end on the third page and cuts the story short to do it.) But the zero draft may have been necessary just to give the writer something to work from, some general mass of material to reshape; a discovery draft can help you discover what you don't want in the paper as much as what you do want.

Another point to be made is that this outlining reveals problems of structure and suggests ways of reorganizing the paper. Because he ends up condensing paragraphs 2 through 7 into one new paragraph 2, throwing out paragraphs 8 and 9, reducing paragraph 10 as paragraph 3, and expanding paragraph 12 into paragraphs 4 through 9, it has been unnecessary for him to worry very much about the sentence-level revisions the original draft might have needed. Now that he has settled on a structure in the second draft, he can begin to focus on sentence-level revisions: eliminating repetition, adding details of description and narration, smoothing unwieldy phrases, clarifying transitions—all the work that makes revision so rewarding and which in the zero draft would not have solved the problems of structure. It is still a very rough draft, but he has given himself a good base to work from.

Write a Journal Entry

Another strategy to assess what you have accomplished so far might be to react to the draft by writing a log entry or a journal entry, talking to yourself about what you hope to accomplish and what you think you have accomplished so far. Often these kinds of dialogues with yourself can lead you to work through problems of structure, arrangement, logic, or emphasis. When you do go back to the actual draft, you may have a clearer sense of how to revise it. As an example, note the following journal entry written after an early draft of a paper recalling a student's performance on stage in high school and what it meant to her to be able to perform in front of hundreds of people.

JOURNAL ENTRY

As I read my paper, I see that I could add better transitions between paragraphs. I could do this by telling what else is going on besides what I am doing. I could tell about the other acts and how I felt watching them.

I could also add more detail about how I felt during the song and the other reactions I had to the audience.

I could tell how I had to get a certain mental state to do this—and to keep from laughing.

Overall, a little more detail about my performance on stage and a little more explanation of how I felt would be beneficial to this paper. I am happy with how it has come along so far but I would like to be able to show the reader exactly how I felt so that they could be more involved.

Writing the journal entry gives her some specific tasks to attend to in the revising. In addition to logs and journal entries, unsent letters can also be helpful because attempting to explain to someone else what you're up to forces you to find other ways of expressing your ideas, which in turn helps you get a handle on them.

Talk About It

Conversation can help with revising whether or not the other person gives any advice or even reacts at all. Sometimes all we need is a sounding board, a sympathetic ear toward which we can direct spontaneous, extemporaneous reflection. Explain to someone else what you have done in the paper, what you hoped to do, what you might do to revise it. You can also talk to yourself, as Nancy Sommers says she does:

> Between drafts, I take lots of showers, hot showers, talking to myself as I watch the water play against the gestures of my hands. In the shower, I get lost in the steam. There I stand without my badges of authority. I begin an imagined conversation with my colleague, the one whom I told in the parking lot of the grocery store, "Oh, but you must read Foucault." I revise our conversation. This time I listen. . . . (28)

The talking will surface realizations about the ideas, language, perspective, structure, organization, and content of the draft that mere solitary, unspoken, or unwritten reflection will never do.

Engage the Work as a Whole

Once you have assessed what you have accomplished in some way and return to the draft itself, try to engage it as a whole work (even if it is only a loose assemblage of parts at the moment). There are a number of ways to do this:

- Read the draft aloud all the way through, from start to finish, stopping only to make check marks where something sounds wrong, seems unclear, or does not work. In both "global" structural matters and "local" stylistic matters, oral reading often surfaces difficulties that silent reading overlooks, particularly in regard to the sequencing of ideas and the clarity of sentences. If you have difficulty following the train of thought or the syntax in certain places, obviously you will need to attend to them in revision.

- Have another person read the draft aloud to you and jot down your reactions to what you hear. Afterward, read your list of the things you noticed to your reader and see if that person has anything else to add that he noticed trying to read it orally. This strategy obviously would work well with a fellow writer or a classmate with whom you could reciprocate by reading his writing aloud.

- Read the draft through silently, making notes in the margins where you feel particular attention will need to be given later on and identifying the kind of attention you think it will need. Bracket or cross out sections you think might be dropped altogether.

- Read the draft through silently, numbering the paragraphs in order and jotting down a phrase or sentence that summarizes what each paragraph is about (as we did with the waterskiing drafts). If you can quote a sentence or a portion of a sentence from each paragraph, so much the better. Afterward, use the numbered list of jottings to draw up an outline of the draft you have actually written. Ask yourself if the pattern that emerges makes sense to you, if the balance between paragraphs is appropriate and desirable given the subject you are working on and the point you want to make, and if the weight of individual sections is proportionate to the overall structure.

All these strategies review the text as a whole and prepare you for revising. You can use more than one of them on a draft and also react to these preliminaries in logs or journals before beginning to revise. By reviewing the draft before revising you discern areas that need attention and are able to break down the task of revision in specific, local subtasks. Of equal importance, you get a sense of what *doesn't* need to be accomplished, either because it's fine as it stands or because it should be discarded rather than revised.

The question of overall structure is important. It makes sense to work on larger issues before working on smaller ones; close and painstaking revision of individual sentences is a waste of time if eventually you have to throw out the entire page. Realistically, of course, one has to expect that sometimes the pages you work hardest at simply have to be discarded in the end and at those times often it is the hard work itself that makes you realize that. Still, if you can concern yourself with organization and development at the beginning, you can often reduce unnecessary revision of individual sentences.

What to Attend to in Revision

However you approach your initial review of the draft's structure, there are virtually universal elements to attend to.

- Make certain you understand the organizing principle of the draft, the reasons behind the decisions you have made about what material has been included and the order in which it has been presented. Writers tend to include elements for a host of reasons that don't always serve the overall structure or the general point of the draft. Essayist Noel Perrin once pointed out an item in an essay of his that was not important information for the general reader or a vital contribution to its theme but had been included in hopes that one potential reader might react to it; it was worth it to him at that point to insert something unrelated to his organizing principle. The point is to know why certain elements have been added and whether they support or conflict with the central principle. When you know that, you can decide what to keep and what to discard or replace. One way to confront the organization is reorganization: describing the need to overcome the "hypnosis" of one's own voice, John Jerome says, "I sometimes read the pages out of order, even read the sentences in reverse order—from the bottom of the page up—just to jar myself out of this overfamiliarity" (111). On the computer he will sometimes move sentences around, seeing if they will go better elsewhere (38); other writers cut up sections of a typed or longhand draft and shuffle their reading sequence to discover what differences different structures make, which is preferable, and what parts seem superfluous or irrelevant.

- Make certain that the beginning and the ending of a piece are both related to the material in the center. One way to do that is to read the piece through, then reread the beginning immediately. Usually the beginning and the ending ought to be connected in some discernible way, whether tightly or loosely. Often it is clearer how the beginning or the ending is related to the center, because the center leads *from* the beginning and leads *into* the ending, but it may be less clear how the beginning and the ending are related to one another because the nature of the center has changed in the drafting. More often than not, the beginning needs to be revised to make it better prepare the reader for the center and the ending; as Annie Dillard says, "Usually I end up throwing away the beginning: the first part of a poem, the first few pages of an essay. It's not holy writ" ("How" 17). But it can also happen that the draft has gotten away from the writer and diverged from a beginning that was preferable to the piece as written; in that case the center and ending will need the major work. In essence there are three questions to be answered here: Does the beginning really begin the draft you actually wrote? Does the ending really end the draft you actually wrote? Are the beginning, the center, and the ending all vitally linked parts of a focused whole?

- Make certain that the center of the piece is sufficiently developed. Clearly I am speaking in the most general terms here, but development is a relative matter. Compositions can be overdeveloped, underdeveloped, or balanced, and the question of appropriate development depends on the topic, the constraints on text form and length imposed by submission guidelines or assignment requirements, and the audience you hope to reach. In the waterskiing drafts, the description of the tournament in the first draft is undeveloped, and the description in the second draft is more thoroughly developed. Generally the questions to ask yourself are, first, whether the information provided is appropriately detailed and concrete for the depth in which you intend to treat the subject and to which the reader needs to be taken and, second, whether the development is sufficient to support the assertions you make, ideas you propose, or conclusions you reach. As before, you need to look at the center for its relationship to the beginning and the ending.

• Make certain you understand the sequence of the development and the ways ideas, paragraphs, and sentences are related to one another. In the main this is the task of examining transitions and connections, the phrases and sentences that link ideas or lead from one paragraph to the next. Asking yourself whether the reader can see why this particular paragraph follows the preceding one or why this particular sentence is succeeded by the one following it. It may mean looking at individual paragraphs and determining their structure, shifting some around to make the development ideas clearer or smoother or more logical and eliminating, adding, or replacing some. (For an example of shifting the position of paragraphs, see Figure 5-1, later in this chapter.)

• Make certain you are satisfied with the way each sentence sounds. To get the sound of the sentence you may have to read it aloud to a real or imaginary listener. If you have any doubts about whether that listener can follow the sense and the syntax (structure) of the sentence, work on the sentence to make it clearer. Most wordsmiths argue that changes in style are usually changes in content for them and generally that is true. The more you work on making certain your sentences make sense, the more likely it is that they will be clear and correct syntactically. Much murkiness and error on the sentence level is the result of murkiness on the conceptual level. One way of getting at the conceptual level is to consult other readers; technical writer Connie Leas, as she worked on a computer-program instruction manual, often went to experienced users of the program to check with them about whether her descriptions and instructions made sense or were easy to follow, then used their reactions to guide much of her revising. Other writers simply have to write down various versions of a sentence to see how it looks on the page and then pick the version that best does the job.

- Make certain that you keep coming back to the entire composition. All the components of the draft should serve the composition in its entirety. The more often you keep yourself in touch with the whole piece, the more the work on its parts will connect with the whole.

- If you make extensive revisions to a draft, prepare a new clean copy and read it through carefully to make certain you understand the revisions and have actually deleted and added the portions of the text you meant to change. Revisions can become confusing and lead to strange text. A concluding sentence of my book on Thomas Southerne reads: "No *really complete* understanding of Restoration drama, particularly in the 1690s, can be *complete* without reading his work ..." (italics added); I had intended to change "can be had" in the original to "can be complete" and "no really complete" to "no real" ("No really complete understanding ... can be had" to "No real understanding ... can be complete"), but fumbled the alteration in execution and am permanently stuck with a mutant version in print. A careful final reading of clean copy uncovers many such errors in transcription.

To follow through on some of this general advice, you might look back at the two drafts of the waterskiing paper in this chapter or ahead to chapter 7, where we will follow a couple of wordsmiths through work on a single project. For the present we can also consider two other samples, one a section of a research paper carried through several drafts, the other a revision of an essay we have followed through several chapters.

The Growth of a Section of a Research Paper

We can learn something about progressive revision in the following series of excerpts from a paper describing critical reviews of *C. S. Lewis: A Biography* by A. N. Wilson. The student had gath-

ered together several reviews of the book, including those mentioned in the excerpts by Richard Brookhiser, John Elson, Gilbert
Meilaender, and F. P. Riga. By highlighting and underlining photocopies of the reviews she knew the most important points each
critic had made and began to write a comparative paper explaining critical reaction to the biography. In the middle of her earliest
draft (she calls it her zero draft) she included the following paragraph:

One agreement among the critics is that the book lacks
logic and believability. One says that the biography "shows certain signs of haste" and that parts of the book that Wilson thought
to be most important are hard to understand (Brookhiser 62).
Another critic also noticed signs of haste when it became apparent that Wilson had only mentioned Lewis's most powerful book
twice, which made it seem like Wilson was in a hurry to finish,
causing serious oversights (Meilaender 525). Meilaender also
says that "the longer one ponders Wilson's narrative the more
difficult it becomes to grasp its logic" (528). Riga explains that
Wilson's ideas are highly speculative and that he has taken many
risks in these speculations that "seem ill-advised or just plain
wrong" (116). John Elson also briefly mentions speculations that
Wilson has made (A3).

The paragraph was a place to bring together references to the believability and logic of Wilson's book, and she wrote a second
draft where she left the paragraph exactly the way she had written it while she concentrated on other aspects of the paper. But
when she began to revise the second draft, she realized that not
everything in the paragraph dealt with believability and logic and
began to separate her ideas a little more. In the third draft she
wrote:

One agreement among some of the critics is that the book
seemed to be written in haste. Brookhiser noted that some parts
of the book that Wilson thought to be most important were not
explained well, and therefore hard to understand (62). Another

critic also noticed signs of haste when it became apparent that Wilson had only mentioned Lewis's most powerful book twice, which made it seem like Wilson was in a hurry to finish, causing serious oversights (Meilaender 525).

Another problem often mentioned by critics is that of believability and logic. Riga explains that Wilson's ideas are highly speculative and that he has taken many risks in these speculations that "seem ill-advised or just plain wrong" (116). John Elson also briefly mentions speculations that Wilson has made (A3). One critic says that "the longer one ponders Wilson's narrative, the more difficult it becomes to grasp its logic" (Meilaender 528).

She had realized that some of the comments were really about the perceived hastiness of the book rather than believability and logic and therefore created two paragraphs where she had had one. Throughout the revision process she kept talking to other group members in the class about her paper and kept going back to the original collection of reviews to keep checking how she was using quotes and paraphrases with her own original sentences. This led her to see that the question of tone had come up in the reviews and she had ignored it so far, so in her fourth draft she pieced in a paragraph on tone after the one on haste, the best place for it to go in her view. She also decided that believability and logic as she was using the terms really referred to the same thing and made the last paragraph in this sequence only about believability. In the fifth and final draft she changed two sentences a little and prepared a presentation text that read:

One agreement among some of the critics is that the book seemed to have been written in haste. Brookhiser notes that some parts of the book that Wilson thought to be most important are not explained well, and therefore hard to understand (62). Another critic also noticed signs of haste when it became apparent that Wilson had only mentioned Lewis's most powerful book twice, which made it seem like Wilson was in a hurry to finish, causing serious oversights (Meilaender 525).

Two critics state a specific problem with the tone. Brookhiser says that "too often his tone, which is meant to be conversational, slides into chattiness" (62). Another critic says that Wilson's book is enjoyable to read, but his tone often becomes "snide and condescending" and that "very few people are mentioned without that tone of voice creeping through" (Meilaender 528).

Believability is the major area of concern that troubles the critics. Riga explains that Wilson's ideas are highly speculative and that he takes many risks in these speculations that "seem ill-advised or just plain wrong" (116). Another critic also mentions Wilson's theories about Lewis's personal life (Elson A3). Riga states that these arguable judgments made about Lewis in Wilson's biography will lead readers to question the validity of the book (116).

Her progress through this section of her paper illustrates her progress through the entire paper and through other papers in the course, the slow build-up of detail through reinterpretation and shuffling of the parts to get a better sequence of details and a more thorough and accurate reading of her source materials. Without the continual rereading and revising, her paper would have been shallower and the information she gives about critical reaction to the biography less comprehensive. Her work on revision helps her to understand what she is writing about as well as helps her make it clearer and more detailed for a reader.

Revising the Hitchhiker Essay

The hitchhiker essay began as a journal entry and progressed through several drafts. The final draft emerged from an important round of revision (see Figure 5-1). This draft has undergone one further set of revisions by hand from the draft in chapter 4; this example is the typed version of that third draft with a fourth set of revisions in longhand. I had dropped the first title, "Learning from a Hitchhiker," as too dull, adopted "The Hitchhiker's Travel Guide" as a catchy play on *The Hitchhiker's Guide to the Galaxy*, then playing on local radio, and then settled on "Traveling Without Baggage," because it was richer and more ironic—the hitchhiker was physically traveling light (without luggage), and metaphori-

cally traveling light (without baggage), and by the end of the
piece I too was traveling without cares and responsibilities. Moreover, I had realized that this was the theme of the piece, the organizing principle: I wanted to show how this hitchhiker made me
realize that I could be more free, less controlled, about enjoying
experience. To do that I wanted to give readers a sense of her
personality in contrast to mine and a sense of the change in my
outlook to be more like hers—that's why I adopted her phrase
("They really freaked me out") at the end of the piece.

In this typed draft I have an introductory section that gets
the reader immediately in the car meeting the hitchhiker and seeing my reaction to her (paragraphs 1, 2, 3), a section about my attitude toward travel (paragraph 4), a section about her attitude
toward travel and vacations (paragraphs 5 and 6), a section about
her current trip (paragraphs 7 and 8), a section in which we go
our separate ways and a comparison is made between us (paragraphs 9 and 10), and a conclusion in which I reveal a change in
my attitude and outlook (paragraph 11). In longhand I marked a
shift that moved paragraph 4 ahead of the first three paragraphs,
because I wanted to present the hitchhiker without that interrup-
tion and make the opening paragraph more of a contrast both
with the paragraph that closes the part where she travels with me
and with the concluding paragraph. It also occurred to me that
paragraphs 5 and 6 went together as one paragraph because of
their unity of focus. Some of the sentence changes are additions
of detail to be more specific (paragraph 4: "and I felt guilty about
leaving ungraded papers behind") or clearer about what was hap-
pening (paragraph 9: "without the sense of urgency I had had on
the Interstate"). Some changes were to alter the response the
reader might have; saying in paragraph 8 that "She was distracted
by the RenCen" seemed more negative an image of her than "She
was more interested in the Renaissance Center"; saying in paragraph 7 "I kept astonishment out of my voice" did not explain
what I was feeling or make enough contrast between us, so I
changed it to "I restrained an instinct to give paternalistic advice,"
which also made me seem a stuffier, more mature person than
she was, an image I wanted to convey. Paragraph 10 still needed
the most work, because it was the one that got at what this all
meant, and so I had the most changes in it, finally throwing out a
line that had been with me since the original journal entry and

Traveling Without Baggage

1   The red-headed hitchhiker ~~was cheerful and chatty from~~ *in the passenger seat, a parttime musician*
was cheerful and chatty. When
~~the moment~~ I picked ~~her~~ up on I-75 south of Flint. We
passed the exit for Oakland University, ~~and~~ I told her a
college friend of mine was teaching there, *someone I hadn't seen for years.*

2   "You ought to go sit in one of his classes," she said. "It
would really freak him out." The thought delighted her.

3   I smiled, *more* ~~as much~~ at her ~~pleasure as the thought of~~ *delight than at his possible surprise.*
~~surprising my friend, "Football". She was a pleasant~~
~~surprise.~~

4   *Even though* I was on my way to spend the night with friends in
Grosse Pointe, *I still drove* ~~driving~~ with the grim determination of
someone going to a business meeting, ~~feeling guilty about~~
~~leaving ungraded papers behind. In three years~~ I'd ~~never~~ *It had been   since*
traveled for *pleasure, not* ~~personal reasons,~~ only for reasons connected
with my teaching, *and I felt guilty about leaving ungraded papers behind.*

5   ~~My hitchhiker, a parttime musician,~~ *She* hadn't traveled
much lately either, partly because of weekend work but
also because, as she said, "Seems like I'm always living
with some dude and can't really have a vacation." *But*

6   She took disappointment lightly, with only a few words
of regret. "A friend was going to travel with me this
weekend, but his wife wouldn't let him. It's really a
bummer." I nodded sympathetically.

FIGURE 5-1. Revised Draft

She was headed for Canada for the weekend, with no   7

destination in mind and only $2.35 in her jeans. I ~~kept~~

restrained an instinct to give paternalistic advice and

~~astonishment out of my voice as I~~ asked how she could

make it through the weekend on so little.

She shrugged "Oh,

"~~Oh,~~ ^s something will turn up. Maybe I'll get a gig in   8

more interested in staring at the

Windsor for the night." She was ~~distracted by the~~

Renaissance Center

~~RenCen~~ and said it really freaked her out.

briskly

I let her out near the tunnel to Canada. She went off ^   9

toward unplanned adventure; I drove away toward my

without the sense of urgency I had had on the Interstate.

safe haven in Grosse Pointe,

She seemed like a somewhat foolhardy, somewhat

~~I might have written her off as a~~ flaky flower-child, but   10

she made me   *always traveled cautiously, clinging to my luggage of*

~~I began to~~ wonder why I ~~chained myself with worry over~~

daily obligations and

~~expenses and~~ responsibilities while she could dare the

world on $2.35. ~~Perhaps she was foolhardy, but was I so~~

~~afraid of life that I needed safety measures all around~~

~~me?~~

Two weeks later I camped alone on the Leelanau   11

I slept a few yards from Lake Michigan; I strolled beach and forest.

Peninsula, ~~strolling beach and forests, sleeping a few~~

~~yards from Lake Michigan.~~ I even climbed Sleeping Bear

Dunes. They really freaked me out.

FIGURE 5-1. (continued)

making the meaning of the title clearer by changing "chained myself with worry over expenses" to "always traveled cautiously,
clinging to my luggage of daily obligations." Sometimes the changes
are just for the sound, as in paragraph 8 where two sentences
switch places or in paragraph 11, where two phrases reverse position. Retyped and a presentation text prepared, this is the version that was eventually published (see Figure 5-2).

Traveling light, daring the world

Even though I was on my way to spend the night with friends in Grosse Pointe, I drove with the grim determination of someone going to a business meeting. It had been years since I'd traveled for pleasure, rather than for reasons connected with teaching, and I felt guilty leaving ungraded papers behind.

The red-haired hitchhiker in the passenger seat, a part-time musician I picked up on I-75 south of Flint, was cheerful and chatty. When we passed the Oakland University exit, I told her a college friend I hadn't seen for years was teaching there.

"You ought to go sit in one of his classes," she said. "It would really freak him out." The thought delighted her and I smiled, more at her pleasure than at his possible surprise.

She hadn't traveled much lately, either. "Seems like I'm always living with some dude and can't really have a vacation," she said. But she took disappointment lightly, with only a few words of regret. "A friend was going to travel with me this weekend," she said later, "but his wife wouldn't let him. It's really a bummer." I nodded sympathetically.

She was headed for Canada for the weekend, with no destination in mind and only $2.35 in her jeans. I restrained an instinct to give paternalistic advice and asked how she could make it through the weekend on so little.

"Oh, maybe I'll get a gig in Windsor for the night." She shrugged. "Something will turn up." She was more interested in staring at the RenCen and said it really freaked her out.

I let her out near the river. She went off briskly toward unplanned adventure; I drove away toward Grosse Pointe, without the sense of urgency I had before on the interstate.

She seemed like a somewhat foolhardy, flaky flower-child, but she made me wonder why I always traveled cautiously, clinging to my luggage of daily obligations and responsibilities, while she could dare the world on $2.35.

Two weeks later I camped alone on the Leelanau Peninsula. I slept a few yards from Lake Michigan and strolled beach and forest. I even climbed the Sleeping Bear Dunes. They really freaked me out.

—*Robert L. Root, Jr.*
Alma

FIGURE 5-2. Published Text

Reaching the Final Draft

Revision is seldom painless, but most often it is rewarding work. The original draft starts getting better before your eyes, perhaps richer, deeper, clearer. Often you need to go through the revision process again and again—starting with a global overview and working on the portions that demand attention during each complete reading. In the end, you have to return to yet another entire reading, one where the words and ideas on the page satisfy you enough that you feel it needs no more revising, that it says what you want it to say in a way that will be clearly understood (and hopefully acceptable) to the reader for whom you intend it (even if that reader is only yourself). Only then should you worry about the quality of the presentation text.

In practice the final draft that emerges from thorough revision is, very often, also the presentation text submitted for publication or grading. Simply in the course of drafting and revising repeatedly the writer tends to correct as she goes along. But, also in practice, almost nobody can safely rely on the process of revision creating both final revised draft and presentation text. For that reason, the preparation of presentation text is best considered as a separate subprocess of composing. As with other subprocesses, to gain some objectivity and distance, the revised draft ideally ought to be set aside for a few hours or days before the preparation of a presentation copy begins. In the next chapter we will consider what that preparation involves.

6 GOING PUBLIC

Up to this point I have been continually reminding you that composing is a recursive action, a jumble of processes and subprocesses that continually interrupt one another and work themselves out in a series of loops and switchbacks and rereading and reacting. In spite of the sequence of the preceding chapters— string-saving, starting, drafting, revising—I have been insisting that the composing process in practice is not really linear (or strictly sequential) and that any writer who tries to complete one subprocess before moving on to another will probably quickly become frustrated. Even the composing subprocess in this chapter—going public—can be recursive; often the preparation of text calls for further revision of a sentence or a paragraph or a section, because you see the text in a new way.

But in the main I *do* want to treat going public as something separate from composing, to be done after the composing is completed. By preparation of presentation text I mean creating the clean, correct copy to present to another person, whether it is a teacher, editor, publisher, or potential reader of a self-published work. When manuscripts are accepted for publication, often someone other than, or in addition to, the author will be required to line-edit or proofread the work. For the publisher to make certain that the copy is correct before it goes off to the printer and for the printer to make certain the "proof" is free of error before running off hundreds or thousands of copies, careful line-by-line editing and word-by-word proofreading need to be done. Publishers and printers know—and writers ought to know—that good line editing and good proofreading take concentration and attention to the task and are most successfully performed when the person doing them is not simultaneously attending to something else. Concentrating on style and sense (the business of drafting and revising) distracts the reader from line editing and proofreading (the business of text preparation). *Composing* the text is a creative act, *going public* with it is chiefly a clerical task; the distinction is one between making meaning and preparing a presentational copy of the final draft.

The Importance of Separating Text Preparation from Composing

The first reason for separating composing from text preparation is a practical one—if you do, you will create a better presentational copy. As much as it may be true that issues of written conformity in spelling, punctuation, grammar, and usage are not indications of a writer's powers of intellect or expression, it is also true that many readers are so distracted by nonconformity that engaging in conformity is worth the writer's while. This is particularly true if the reader to whom you are delivering the piece is someone who decides whether you will be published or paid or given a passing grade.

However, having a presentation text is also important for the writer, because the writer is one of the readers affected by the state of the manuscript. Composition teacher Elizabeth Bell, accustomed to writing on a word processor, found herself on one occasion having to draft and revise in longhand and was dismayed to discover how difficult it was to follow her own manuscript:

> I found myself frustrated by thumbing through pages of messed up, marked out, arrow-laden prose in search of a train of thought that sounded logical in my head, but appeared—when I could find it at all—fragmented and haphazard on the written page. (6)

The word processor, she finds, allows her "to see my work as a clean-copy whole, no matter at what stage of composing I am";

consequently she has a better sense of what she has accomplished in the draft and where she needs more work. She writes that "the process of being able to see and read one's work-in-progress without surface-level distractions can change one's relationship to the writing" and compares the discovery to her own experience as a writing teacher:

> Any teacher who has read stacks of student papers knows that the neatly written papers, especially if they come toward the end of the stack, enjoy a more kindly reception than their illegible, coffee-stained, more hapless colleagues. Whether or not the appearance of the paper ultimately affects our evaluation of the writing, it certainly affects the way we read it. The same, I discovered, is true of our own writing. Our way of reading our own writing—and perhaps our understanding of the purpose for doing it—changes when we are more immediately able to concentrate on its substantive levels instead of its accidental ones. (7)

If the state of the manuscript interferes with the reading for the writer herself, it must have a greater impact on a reader unfamiliar with the work.

John Jerome corroborates Elizabeth Bell's experience when he writes that "one of the more shocking events in electronic writing" occurs when he works on a printout of his draft. "I'll have the text as close to perfect as I think I can get it, will think it ready to send. Then the paper copy will expose how awkward and unfinished it really is" (111). The visual dimension of writing is more important than we sometimes realize, and clean hard copy helps us see past the surface to the substance below. By contrast, some word-processing features, such as variable typefaces and justified right margins, may be distracting even in correct copy; as Jerome says: "The writer wants the editor paying attention to the thinking, not the spaces between and around words" (125).

The second reason for separating composing from text preparation may seem to be less practical and more idealistic (although I would argue that it is equally practical): Writing ought to do the writer's business first and foremost, before it does anybody else's business. There may be exceptions to that rule—garbage disposer installation manuals and VCR operating instructions, for example—but in general the writer ought to write for himself even when writing something assigned by another person. At first glance, this may seem contradictory or paradoxical, but if you have not invested some portion of yourself into your writing, you are likely to produce work that is, at best, superficial, trivial, or perfunctory. There may be teachers who prefer banal correctness over haphazard significance—and undoubtedly there are—but most prefer their student writers to make a commitment to the writing project and are willing to be flexible in evaluation to accommodate commitment. Moreover, there are real consequences to seeing a writing project as someone else's rather than your own. Connie Leas, a technical writer, has told of a writer she knew who put together an instruction manual for the United States Army made up of parts boilerplated together from other writing he had done. When military mechanics attempted to follow his manual to make repairs to truck engines, they found the instructions to be wrong, irrelevant to the kind of engine they were working on, and consequently they could not fix them. The writer here surely had to worry about how well his writing served his reading, but he also had to have enough commitment to the project to understand what he was writing for himself. The two go together.

Composing, through all its prewriting, drafting, and revising, is complete when the writer has discovered what she wants to say and has said it to a degree of development, clarity, and style that satisfies herself (given the circumstances of the situation). Going public is a separate action because in some cases it's an unnecessary one—you don't need to be published to have said what you wanted to say as well as you hoped to say it. Most practicing wordsmiths, no matter how successful they have been at writing, have accumulated a pile of rejection slips over the years. Only a relative handful of professional writers ever reach the point where no one rejects anything they write. The experience of searching for a publisher teaches them that publishing is more often a question of finding a receptive reader than it is a question of somehow composing a universally acceptable text. Readers each bring to what they read their own backgrounds and assumptions; so too do editors and publishers and teachers. Getting the approval of readers sometimes requires waiting until the right readers come along; getting the approval of yourself requires only working on a piece until it satisfies you enough for you to accept it as it is whether you ever go public with it or not.

Preparing Academic Presentation Texts

At first preparing papers for publishers and preparing papers for teachers may seem like quite different tasks—the person trying to publish has probably chosen a writing life, for one thing—but in reality the circumstances are very much the same. Publishers and teachers are both willing to provide guidelines for the prospective writer; both can be consulted about expectations for manuscript preparation. In both cases a writer satisfies expectations more readily with each successive successful manuscript; having learned what worked in one piece the writer incorporates those elements into another and another until they recur almost automatically. Anyone who has waited for the first assignment in a course to be returned by the teacher knows the anxiety of that wait—this is the moment when you learn how well you interpreted the teacher's expectations, when you discover what needs to be done to adjust your approach to the subject on the next paper to get nearer the teacher's expectations than you did this time. Because a good many academic papers are expected to be the same kind of paper generally, particularly within a given content area, most students can improve (with application) over a series of courses and teachers—the expectations generally are not so widely divergent as to be unique to each individual case.

The basic rule of thumb in preparing academic texts is: *Always prepare the text as if it were assigned by the most demanding teacher*. If you try to satisfy the expectations of the most demanding reader, you will always satisfy the expectations of the least demanding. The corollary to that rule is: *Always work from the clearest possible sense of what specifically is being demanded of a presentation text by the person to whom you intend to submit it*. Academic journals usually publish the names of the style manuals they want contributors to follow ("the third edition of the *Publication Manual* of the American Psychological Association"; "the current edition of *The MLA Handbook*"); many publications will provide "instructions for authors" upon request; many publishers (such as Macmillan) publish their own guides for contracted authors; many teachers specify formats they want papers to follow and style manuals to be used in assignments—those who do not should be asked directly what they expect. A good handbook covering both MLA and APA styles usually covers most academic assignment requirements.

Strategies for Preparing Presentation Text

Going public then is preparing a presentation copy of the final draft and submitting it for the reaction, recognition, and/or evaluation of other readers—editors, publishers, teachers, audiences. Consider the following as you prepare a presentation text:

- Plan time in which to prepare text as a separate activity. Just as with revising set aside the final draft for at least twenty-four hours, having satisfied yourself that the content and expression of the draft are where you want them to be. When you read it to prepare a presentation text, try to read only for text preparation matters—spelling, punctuation, paragraphing, documentation format, capitalization, titles, pagination, boldfacing, underlining, and italics.
- Read the manuscript word for word. In reading for sense we tend to read in chunks of material, skimming sections and instantaneously surveying subsections, settling for the gist of a paragraph rather than following the sequence of words linearly. But the text preparer cannot afford to read that way, as an interested reader. Reading word for word surfaces problems of grammar and syntax, spelling, punctuation, and typing.

    One good way of making certain you read every word is to read it aloud, particularly to another person. For example, read aloud this sentence from the second draft of the waterskiing paper in chapter 5: "As the boat turned around to come back through, I was thinking that the speed the boat would be speeding up to was a speed that I never had made it through at before." If you hadn't noticed the repetition of the word "speed" during sight reading, you would during an oral reading, as well as the awkwardness of "never had made it through at before." You could then change the sentence to something that calls less attention to its syntax and more attention to its ideas: "As the boat turned around and started toward the buoys again, I realized that it would be taking me through at a speed I had never skiied before" or "We turned around and the boat sped up, going faster than I had ever skied before." Either of these read aloud would sound better.

Writing groups often use this approach, allowing the writer to read aloud to several other people and letting their questions and comments guide revision or, in this case, editing. The writer takes responsibility for the proofreading. Often students who are having difficulty with text preparation discover their problems immediately by reading the text aloud. As in revision, so in text preparation, the perspective of another person can be valuable. An alternative is to have someone else read a copy of the writer's draft aloud; the writer gets a sense of how the sentences sound and can observe the places where the reader has trouble following the text. A third alternative is to use a reliable friend, classmate, or relative as a line editor/proofreader.

- Read the manuscript with text preparation materials at hand. The text preparation materials would include a dictionary, a handbook of usage, any guidelines from the publisher or instructor, any style sheet or manual for documentation required by the project. Everybody needs to consult a dictionary or handbook from time to time, even people whose word processors have built-in spelling and grammar checkers. Guidelines from the publisher or instructor can change the rules by insisting on one specific documentation form over another (for example, MLA or APA) or simply by having their own idiosyncratic format (for example, one publisher insists that punctuation after underlined titles be underlined also, whereas another insists that punctuation should never be underlined).
- Read the manuscript for documentation separately from your reading for other matters. Formats for citing references are largely arbitrary, following no natural laws of

language or usage; however, they do tend to be consistent within individual systems. The easiest way to make your documentation conform to the prescribed format is to perform a check of the documentation in your draft in consultation with the appropriate style sheet or manual, as a separate action apart from the other text preparation you do. Identify the kind of citation you have and compare it item by item with the corresponding citation in the style sheet, making yours conform to the style sheet.

- Recognize that some text preparation problems surface only when preparing text, because text preparation is a clerical act, not a creative act. For example, in typing out handouts for my classes I routinely type "form" for "from" and "specualtion" for "speculation." This kind of metathesis is not evidence of misspelling but evidence of mistyping, just as when my students type "the" as "tje." Knowing that I know how to spell "from" and "speculation" is not sufficient for my text preparation; I have to read text as if I didn't know these things, because they will surface in my final copy despite my knowledge unless I do.

- If you retype an entire page to correct some errors, reread the entire page, not just the place where the errors occurred. The problem with extensive retyping is that it provides new opportunities for error. The advantage that word processors have over typewriters is their ability to make corrections without extensive retyping of correct text, but even there it is necessary to reread. The word processor has created a whole new class of textual error, often caused by the editor's failure to *delete* old material at the same time that he *inserts* new material. Your local newspaper will daily provide examples of this kind of text preparation error.

- Edit and proofread from clean hard copy. Some people are very good at revising and editing from a computer screen, but many mistakes that show up in printouts are the kind not easily detected on the screen, such as misplaced or erroneous commands to the printer. Moreover, the end result is supposed to be clean hard copy, and it ought to be checked over as such before being submitted anywhere.

Getting a Background in Going Public

Like so many ideas in this book, the following suggestions for getting a background in going public are flexible, and no writer should use only one approach. Moreover, all of them assume a certain willingness to work at creating a clean, correct presentation text, a certain ability to recognize error, and a certain dexterity with reference tools. Not all writers can be assumed to have those talents at first, and probably those writers who do also have a background in reading published texts (so that they assimilate much of the information about what presentation texts look like) and in writing texts of one kind or another. For those who do not have that background, there are a couple of ways of getting it.

• Read widely in the forms of writing you hope to or are required to produce. What are other people doing in this format? with this subject? for this audience? Moreover, how does the language of those people *sound?* Read some published texts aloud to yourself to get the rhythms of their language in your ear. Copy some of their pages word for word in longhand to force yourself to attend to the smallest units of their sentences.

• React to the text preparation of papers in writing when they are returned to you in academic courses. If you get back a paper where text preparation errors are noted, write a log entry or a journal entry about them, forcing yourself to analyze what they are and how to correct them. Consult a handbook or dictionary, a classmate or friend, or the course instructor, if the problem is not one you really understand. For example, one student wrote the following as part of a journal entry about text preparation errors on one of her papers:

Each and other are two separate words that I always join together. I have to adhere to the concept of spacing between my words. I made this error in my paper: "Because Negaunee was a small town, everybody knew eachother."

Actually, each and other are two separate words that should be written as such.

A sentence fragment was pointed out on my third page of the draft. I wrote this: "Especially crabby mine workers who would come in after the midnight shift." This is not a complete sentence with a subject, predicate, and verb. I could correct this by adding a comma before the fragment instead of starting a new sentence. This is how it would look if I had done it correctly: "Customers sometimes treat waitresses in a rude manner, especially crabby mine workers who come in after the midnight shift." Sentence fragments should be an easy problem to correct, because there are many solutions to revising them.

The only other problem I had was misspelled words, and I just looked those up in the dictionary.

Like other forms of writing, the act of writing logs and journals about text preparation problems is a way not only to solve them but to make you more aware of recurring problems and thus able to eliminate them more readily, perhaps more automatically.

- Create a checklist of the text preparation problems that recur in your drafts. If you have someone reading the text aloud or proofreading generally, note the errors they discover and keep track of them. If you have previous work with comments about text preparation on it—previous submissions or coursework from other teachers—review those comments and add to your checklist. The idea is to discover your particular, recurring problems of text preparation and generate a list of items that you deliberately check either separately from or along with your other proofreading. If some teacher has highlighted your use of the semicolon, check every place you have a semicolon by consulting a usage handbook to see if you are using it as the handbook recommends; if teachers indicate that your paragraphs are generally either too short (one brief sentence) or too long (several pages), check your paragraphs to see where they begin and end and whether they could be either combined or broken up. Whatever the item that has gotten attention in the past, check for it in the present, particularly if it is one that has surfaced repeatedly. Constant, deliberate checking for a problem may help eliminate it; it will certainly remedy it.

- Find an editor to work with you. It may be the course instructor, a roommate or classmate or tutor, a fellow writer or a writing group, a friend, or someone at a writing center. Talking with another person about problems you have had in the past and, in particular, about work-in-progress as it progresses can help give you a better eye for not only what you do badly but also what you do well. Many scholars and teachers like to compare learning to write to learning to do an athletic activity, where individualized work with an experienced and accomplished coach can bring you farther faster than any textbook or series of lectures is likely to do. Just like talking to the golf pro or the batting coach or the aerobics instructor can improve your performance, so conferring with a writing coach can improve your composing. As your experience and skills grow, you will need that one-on-one consulting less and less.

Neal Gabler once commented that he tried to write his film reviews in longhand and save the typing for the final copy, as a reward (Root 203). The reward of clean presentation copy is its neatness, its readability, the crisp black indentations marching across pristine white pages. Most writers have observed that published texts are even more readable somehow, but they have also observed that sometimes you do not spot things you could have said better until they appear in print. The advantage of appearing in print—or in typed presentation texts—frequently is that it trains you to spot things you could have said better earlier, before they appear in print.

So it is with careful text preparation in general. The more often you are conscientious about it, the less often you have to make corrections and changes. But it never becomes something that you can take for granted. Each time a final copy comes back to you, from a publisher or a teacher, review it not only for items they have noted but also for items you might have overlooked, then add them to your checklist. In time you'll notice that the checklist isn't growing very much and that you run through it quickly. You'll also notice that there is never an occasion when you can simply accept your text on faith. Preparing to go public should be a regular stage in your writing.

7 WORDSMITHS AT WORK

Libraries are rich in examples of wordsmiths at work. For example, *Working Days: The Journals of "The Grapes of Wrath,"* written by John Steinbeck and edited by Robert DeMott, gives readers a sense of the evolution of Steinbeck's great novel by recording the progress that he makes on it day by day. The book also reveals that, as systematic and persistent as Steinbeck was in the eventual full draft of the novel, *The Grapes of Wrath* came about only after Steinbeck had written a preliminary essay, edited another man's series of reports on migrant camps, and gone through several stages: a seven-part series of newspaper articles called "The Harvest Gypsies," an unfinished novel called *The Oklahomans*, a completed and then destroyed book-length satire called *L'affair Lettuceberg*, and the final work of his great novel. The book itself did not simply come out of him; it was preceded by immersion in context and various forms of trial runs. Immediately before starting the version that became *The Grapes of Wrath* Steinbeck completed *L'affair Lettuceberg* and then wrote to his agent to explain why he had decided not to publish it. In part he explained, "I had forgotten that I hadn't learned to write books, that I will never learn to write them. . . . I thought I could write easily and that anything I touched would be good simply because I did it. Well any such idea conscious or unconscious has been exploded for some time to come" (Steinbeck xl-xli). By that time

Steinbeck, who was thirty-six, had already published eight books and was about to write his masterpiece.

Two points emerge from Steinbeck's example. One is that good writing is always hard, even for master wordsmiths; the other is that good writing, even for master wordsmiths, emerges out of a process of earlier string-saving, prewriting, and drafting, sometimes all jumbled up together.

I have cited an example of a novelist at work and similar examples abound, but examples of nonfiction writing are also plentiful. For instance, J. Lyndon Shanley's *The Making of "Walden"* is a fascinating study of the ways in which Henry David Thoreau drew on his journals and other material to craft his great work, *Walden, or Life in the Woods.* Donald M. Murray's book *Shop Talk* collects a number of comments writers have made about their processes, most of which reinforce what has been said in the preceding chapters. In this concluding chapter I would like to give some examples of wordsmiths at work taken from my own classes in composition, in part because the processes of professionals are readily available in libraries, in part because these samples represent the attempts of novices to struggle at wordsmithery.

A Wordsmith at Work: Writing About Growing Up

In the first example we get to see a student work through from preliminary explorations to a final draft that is thorough and well developed. The progress of a paper about growing up in his hometown led Brian through a number of activities, drafts, and revisions. He began with the preliminary work in Figure 7-1, a rough map of his hometown and then a list of items the map helped him to recall about growing up. In the course of making the list he discovered a number of memories about the local barbershop and decided that might make a topic worth further exploration. He used the barbershop as the center of a clustering diagram and let himself free-associate memories connected with it (Figure 7-2). The clustering produced all kinds of memories and led him to make a list of what might go in a rough draft about the place (Figure 7-3). The questions at the end of the list help him to

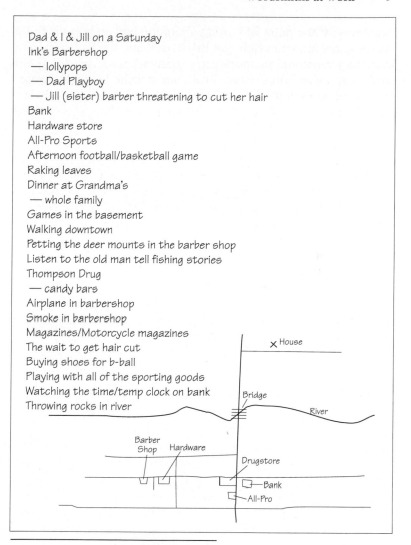

Dad & I & Jill on a Saturday
Ink's Barbershop
— lollypops
— Dad Playboy
— Jill (sister) barber threatening to cut her hair
Bank
Hardware store
All-Pro Sports
Afternoon football/basketball game
Raking leaves
Dinner at Grandma's
— whole family
Games in the basement
Walking downtown
Petting the deer mounts in the barber shop
Listen to the old man tell fishing stories
Thompson Drug
— candy bars
Airplane in barbershop
Smoke in barbershop
Magazines/Motorcycle magazines
The wait to get hair cut
Buying shoes for b-ball
Playing with all of the sporting goods
Watching the time/temp clock on bank
Throwing rocks in river

× House

Bridge

River

Barber
Shop   Hardware

Drugstore

☐—Bank

All-Pro

FIGURE 7-1.   Mapping and Listing

ponder what the point of writing about the barbershop might be. All these preliminaries help get Brian back into the barbershop by drawing long-stored memories to the surface and immersing him in the experience once more. From this start he launches himself into a discovery draft, originally written in longhand.

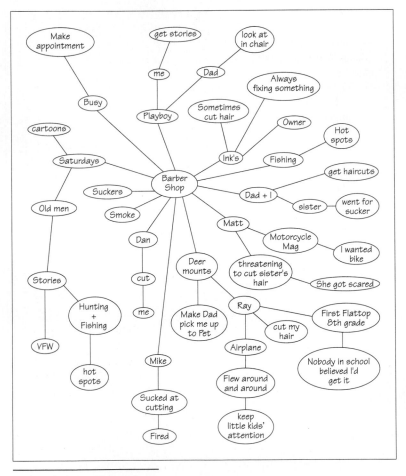

FIGURE 7-2. Clustering

ßSATURDAY MORNINGS IN BARBERSHOP

Things in Shop

Deer Mounts—pet

AIRPLANE—get kids' attention

PLAYBOY—trying to get glances

MOTORCYCLE MAGS—dreaming

OLD MEN —stories   hotspots

CARTOONS—on TV to watch

SMOKE—from cigarettes & cigars & pipes

HAIR ON THE GROUND

BARBERS   MATT, RAY, PETE (OWNER)

How has it affected my life?

What does it do for me? Why do I always enjoy getting my

hair cut there?

Why do I feel at home there?

FIGURE 7-3.   List

ROUGH DRAFT

My Saturdays were always special to me as a young boy. I remember my Dad & I making the trip to Ink's Barber Shop. The day would basically start like all others. We would get up and have breakfast. About 9:00 AM we would either drive or walk down to the barber's shop. Everyone in the shop basically knows each other and says hi. It's sort of like when Norm walks in on Cheers—they all say hi. My dad & I would go in and shake hands and say hello.

Many things inside the shop were very intriguing. I remember the deer mounts on the wall. I would always try to get my dad to lift me up so I could pet them. The eyes of the deer always caught my attention. Whenever my dad was too busy to lift me up

I would stare up at the mounts, until it was my turn to get my hair cut. I would walk all around the shop like I owned it. I thought it was a great place. Magazines in the shop got a great amount of attention from me. Matt, the barber who cut my dad's hair, always had motorcycle magazines for me to look at. I tell all the guys I was going to have a bike as soon as I could. I also remember Playboy. Being a horny little kid I'd walk all over the shop trying to get glances every now and then. The old men would read the newspaper or a hunting or fishing magazine. Since my grandfathers were big fishermen I always was all ears to a fishing story. The old men would smoke their cigs, cigars or pipes. I liked playing with the push button ashtrays. Pete Ink the owner would always come in to fix something and sometimes to cut a person's hair. Ray the barber who cut my hair always did a great job. When I would be running around he would tell me to stay out of the hair on the ground. Ray would always ask me how I wanted my hair cut even though I always got the same thing, every time. Ray had an airplane by his chair that he flew for little boys that cried and sometimes he would fly it for me. It would go round and round. I watched until I got dizzy. Ray's chair was also by the TV. So I got to watch cartoons too. They always had Bugs Bunny on when Dad and I got there. The guys in the shop have affected me greatly in my views. They were always so nice to me and in return I've always been nice to them. Some of the old men in the shop would tell me stories of when my grandpa coached them in college. The barbershop always represented a place I could go and talk about fishing or anything else.

Brian lets his ideas tumble out of him in this draft and doesn't bother to paragraph or organize very much, simply letting the memories flow. In his next draft, also in longhand, he expands on many of the ideas in this draft by adding descriptive details and also tries a conclusion that tells how he still likes to get his hair cut at Ink's Barber Shop. That draft he types up, breaking up the longhand draft into paragraphs, and using the typed draft for more revision after discussion with group members in class about work-in-progress. The revisions are typed into that draft and a fourth version run off and handed in for teacher comments. When the paper comes back, a week or so later, Brian sits down and reads it through, then writes the following journal entry:

The paper sounds good and I like the story a lot. But now being away from it for a while I see a number of problems. The paragraphs that I have written need more details and to be broken down. Some of the paragraphs are too long. They go on and on switching from one subject to the next. I need to watch for this in papers to come. The main way the paper could be strengthened would be through details. The details would help the paper enormously. Adding to the motorcycle magazine will help put a picture in the reader's mind so they could see the bike I was looking at in the magazine. Talking about people in the shop, I need to give names to make them seem tangible to everyone. Just saying old man doesn't help. All you get with old man is a basic picture but using names invokes your imagination. Also to strengthen it would be to break up the paragraphs. This will make the paper flow easier and make easier reading. The main idea is details, talking about objects in the shop in greater depth. I need to paint a picture in the reader's mind with the details. Tell them how Ray's head looked before and after he got a hair piece. Tell the reader about the colors on the airplane by Ray's hair and how it worked. Was the plane loud, did it fly all over the shop or just in one place? Those are the kinds of questions I need to ask myself.

What works with this paper? I need to expand on ideas. Your ideas make total sense after a week layoff and then reading the paper again. I think the paper could be good but needs details. If I break up the paragraphs and add the details the paper will dramatically improve. The paper has to be a photo album in the reader's mind so they can see each and every picture in detail.

Having resolved to change paragraph structure and add details Brian makes longhand revisions in his hard copy and then revises the paper on the word processor. In addition, he runs off a copy, checks it through for text preparation errors, makes a few corrections, and runs one last clean copy, error free, to include in his portfolio of class writing. The final draft reads as follows.

Ink's Barber Shop

My Saturdays were always special to me as young boy. I remember my dad and I making the trip to Ink's Barber Shop. The day would start like all others. We would get up, and I would eat my cereal in front of Bugs Bunny with my sister, Jill. If it was a nice day out we would walk downtown or else we would drive. The trip was about a half mile and did not take long. It was always fun walking across the bridge and running over the railroad tracks in town. It was nice to walk through downtown Kent.

At the barber shop everyone basically knows each other. The barbers would have their silk-looking shirts on and their barber licenses on the mirrors behind them. Now when I think about it, it reminds me of *Cheers* when Norm walks in and everyone says, "Norm." Dad and I would walk around and say "Hi" to everyone and get in line. People from all over Kent came to get their hair cut, like Doug Simms and his boy, David. My uncle Steve would drive my two cousins, Hugh and Ben, in to get their cuts. Ben and David were good friends and would play together in the shop.

To me as a small boy the shop had many temptations. The deer mounted on the wall always caught my attention first. I would beg Dad to lift me up so I could pet the deer. I would always stare at the eyes and touch the nose to see what it felt like. When you petted the hair of the deer it was soft and smooth. Other times when Dad would not lift me up I would stand under the mount and stare up at it. I loved walking all over the shop acting like I owned the place. Basically, I thought I did own it.

Matt, the barber who cut my dad's hair, always had motorcycle magazines for me to look at. Looking at those motorcycle magazines made me want a motorcycle. I thought the sleek-looking race bikes were awesome. I would sit in the chair at the shop and pretend I was riding a motorcycle, revving the RPM's to pop a wheelie and take off. I would tell everyone in the shop I was going to get a bike. The other magazine I vividly remember was *Playboy*. Being a little kid I would wander around the shop hoping to get a glance of a naked woman. If I did get lucky and catch a glance, I could brag for a week straight to my friends.

The shop was always full of smoke from the old men smoking cigarettes. The old men would smoke and read fishing magazines or the newspaper. The shop had these ashtrays with buttons on the top, that would put your cigarette out if you pushed it. I would play with the ashtray forever just pushing that button over and over. While I was doing that the old men would tell me fishing stories or about playing football for Grandpa at Kent State University. I loved to hear stories about Grandpa or fishing.

My barber Ray also wore the silk-looking shirt and he always cut my hair. I would climb into the chair and he would ask me how I wanted my hair cut. But he knew it was always the same, nice and short. Ray always did a great job with my hair, cutting it perfectly. When I was running around the shop Ray would tell me to stay out of the hair on the ground.

I remember one Saturday when Dad and I went to get our hair cut and Ray was not bald anymore. He had hair on top of his head. I could not understand how he got his hair back. I sat there the whole time in the shop wondering how he got his hair back. It came in so quickly and was thick too. I talked myself into believing that because Ray was a barber he could make his hair grow. Ray still today wears a hairpiece and it looks good.

Ray also had a real neat airplane by his chair. He flew the plane for kids that were scared. Since I thought I owned the shop I wasn't scared, but Ray sometimes would turn the plane on anyway for me. Ray's chair was also right by the TV so I got to watch Bugs Bunny while I got my hair cut. When I was finished getting my hair cut Ray made sure I got a sucker. My favorite flavor sucker was lemon-lime.

After Dad and I had both gotten our hair cut, it was time to pay. Dad sometimes would give me the money before we went in the shop so I could pay Ray. Dad told me to always give him an extra dollar as a tip for the good job. After paying Dad and I would say good-bye and head home to show Mom our new haircuts.

Ink's Barber Shop has left me with many fond memories. Whenever I go home to Kent, I always stop in the shop to say "Hi" or to get my hair cut from either Matt, Ray, or the newest barber, Dan, at Ink's Barber Shop.

The portrait of Ink's Barber Shop that emerges from Brian's final draft is affectionate and evocative, but it could not have been achieved without the preliminary work, the multiple drafts with their incremental revisions, the engagement with the writing through the analyzing journal entry, and the allowing for time in which the work could grow.

A Wordsmith at Work: Writing a Research-Based Paper

In the chapter on revising we looked at several versions of a paragraph in a paper reporting on critical reviews of a biography of C. S. Lewis. Our second example of a wordsmith at work returns us to that paper to see two of its five drafts in their entirety and to follow the process of its opening paragraph and concluding sentences through all five drafts.

Melody, the author, had collected several reviews of *C. S. Lewis: A Biography* by A. N. Wilson; she had been motivated to report on reviews of this book by the nature of the assignment and also by her past experience having read and enjoyed books by Lewis. Although the instigation for the research and the resulting paper came from her professor, the actual subject of the paper came out of her own interests and background. Having read Lewis (but not Wilson's biography) she was in a position to be more knowledgeable about what she read and was interested in comparing the reviews as a way of deciding whether to read the biography (a common motive for reading reviews in the first place). On the reviews she photocopied she underlined key sentences or put a brace (}) in the margin identifying material she might use in the paper. Later she went back through the reviews and expressly identified sections she intended to use by writing "quote" next to the brace. With the reviews spread out before her to consult, she wrote what she identified as the "zero draft" of the paper, the draft in which she would discover what she had to work with:

The reviews of the book "C. S. Lewis: A Biography" by A. N. Wilson held mixed reactions. The book gives people a look inside the life of the English writer who wrote such things as "The Chronicles of Narnia," "The Great Divorce," "Surprised by Joy," and many other works.

One important comparison in the reviews of this book was that between Wilson and other authors who have written biographies of C. S. Lewis. One critic claims that Wilson's biography is "clearly the best" but is "not without its difficulties" (Riga 116). Riga states that the biography by R. L. Green and Walter Hooper tended to make some of the more important aspects of Lewis's life seem less important and that of William Griffin failed to write about new material that he had discovered (116). Another critic explains that even though Wilson had not had the personal acquaintance with Lewis that previous biographers (such as Sayer, R. L. Green, and Hooper) had, he does a good job regardless of this with his "detailed, intimate knowledge of two major factors in Lewis's life—Oxford University and English literature" (Aeschliman 54). Yet another critic of Wilson's book is not so generous with praise. Gilbert Meilaender believes that the best biography of Lewis is the one by George Sayer and that Wilson's is "heavy on information, but with almost no interpretative schema" (525).

One agreement among the critics is that the book lacks logic and believability. One says that the biography "shows certain signs of haste" and that parts of the book that Wilson thought to be most important are hard to understand (Brookhiser 62). Another critic made it seem like Wilson was in a hurry to finish, causing serious oversights (Meilaender 525). Meilaender also says that "The longer one ponders Wilson's narrative the more difficult it becomes to grasp its logic" (528). Riga explains that Wilson's ideas are highly speculative and that he has taken many risks in these speculations that "seem ill-advised or just plain wrong" (116). John Elson also briefly mentions speculations that Wilson has made (A3).

Many of the critics mention several faults in the biography that cause them to question its validity. Meilaender explains that what is unique about Wilson's book is that he attempts to analyze the psyche of Lewis, but that Wilson also fails to support his ideas with sufficient factual evidence. When talking about the way that Wilson analyzes Lewis in search for an understanding of him and his relationships with women, the critic says that his evidence used to support his ideas "can't carry the interpretive load Wilson places upon it. The threads form an informative and witty narrative, but the facts do not fully persuade" (Meilaender 528). Riga maintains that the arguable judgements made about Lewis in Wilson's biography were highly speculative and that the risks he took will lead readers to question the validity of the book (116).

The more convincing critics are the ones who do not care for Wilson's biography of Lewis, such as Meilaender. They seem to be more educated with the life of Lewis and offer more information to support their claims. Many of these critics do not agree with Wilson and the way that he attached so much significance to events in Lewis's life that seemed illogical. They also agree that he is guilty of overinterpretation of what made Lewis act in the manner in which he did and write what he did.

The fact that Melody labels this draft a "zero draft" tells us she knows she is on a voyage of discovery here, trying to put into her own words the ideas she has found on the pages of the reviews and trying to quote the reviewers directly when it seems important to let them speak for themselves. Some of the language is awkward and some of the ideas vague, but in a zero draft she doesn't worry about that—those things can be addressed and re-solved during the revisions to follow. For the present she needs to assess what she has and make some decisions about how to work with it.

Rather than reprint all five drafts, I can direct you back to chapter 5 to see how her third paragraph evolves between the zero and final drafts and also demonstrate how a couple of key sections of the piece evolve during the revisions. For example, notice the first paragraph above. When Melody takes a look at her zero draft, she begins to work on not only the language but the ideas in her first paragraph. In her second draft she changes the first paragraph as follows:

The critical reaction to the book *C. S. Lewis: A Biography* by A. N. Wilson was mixed. The critics who reviewed the book were most interested in the believability of it and how it compared to earlier biographies of Lewis. The book gives people a look inside the life of the English writer who wrote such things as "The Chronicles of Narnia," "The Great Divorce," "Surprised by Joy," and many other works.

The changes are stylistic in the first sentence and also concerned with focus. The addition of the second sentence makes the opening paragraph more about the critical reaction to the book and the major emphasis of her report on those reviews than about the subject of the book. In the conclusion she adds another two sentences to her original closing sentence, "They also agree that he is guilty of overinterpretation of what made Lewis act in the manner in which he did and write what he did." It is more of a summary sentence: "Those who liked the book thought it was pleasant to read, although they mentioned faults. It is apparent that if they had perhaps understood the extent of these faults, then they, too, would have disliked the book."

In her third draft she returns to the opening paragraph and makes it much more direct and much more open about what her findings will be.

The critical reviews of the book *C. S. Lewis: A Biography* by A. N. Wilson were both positive and negative, although the more convincing critics were those with unfavorable reviews. The book attempted to probe into the private life of C. S. Lewis in order to analyze the events that shaped his life. The critics were primarily concerned with the believability of the book and whether or not Wilson gave sufficient evidence to support his views.

One common topic in the reviews of the book is the comparison between Wilson's biography and other authors who have written about C. S. Lewis.

The second and third sentences of the previous draft are switched around and rewritten to make the second sentence connect to the subject of the book before the third sentence directs the reader toward the focus of the reviews. She also changes the opening sentence of the second paragraph to smooth the style. Her previous conclusion gets dropped and she substitutes, "They do not agree with the illogical way that Wilson attaches so much significance to events in Lewis's life in order to demystify his personal life and beliefs." It is more direct and informative about what the critics disagree with, and it eliminates the judgment that she had made about what those who liked the book might have thought under different circumstances.

The fourth draft makes fewer changes in the opening paragraph, but one important one is to substitute a new reference to the critics' reaction for the sentence about the critics' concerns and let the opening sentence of the second paragraph introduce the issue of comparison with other biographies.

The critical reviews of the book *C. S. Lewis: A Biography* by A. N. Wilson were both positive and negative, although the more convincing critics were those with unfavorable reviews. The book attempted to probe into the private life of C. S. Lewis in order to analyze the events that shaped his life. It also works to persuade the intellectuals who have put Lewis aside to re-examine him ("Beer and Beatitudes" 81).

One common topic in the reviews of the book is the comparison between Wilson's biography and those of other authors who have written about C. S. Lewis.

In this draft Melody is working on making transitions tighter, sentences clearer and more direct. To conclude the draft, she adds to the final paragraph a quote she had used earlier and then displaced: "'The longer one ponders Wilson's narrative, the more difficult it becomes to grasp its logic' (Meilaender 528)." She only tinkers with the opening of a few paragraphs to make the transitions clearer before running off this draft as her fifth and final draft.

A Report on the Reviews of "C. S. Lewis: A Biography"

The critical reviews of the book *C. S. Lewis: A Biography* by A. N. Wilson were both positive and negative, although the more convincing critics are those with unfavorable reviews. The book attempts to probe into the private life of C. S. Lewis in order to analyze the events that shaped his life. It also works to persuade the intellectuals who have put Lewis aside to re-examine him ("Beer and Beatitudes" 81).

One common topic in the reviews of the book is the comparison between Wilson's biography and those of other authors who have written about C. S. Lewis. F. P. Riga claims that Wilson's biography is "clearly the best" but is "not without its difficulties" (116). He also states that it avoids the faults of other biographies, such as that of R. L. Green and Walter Hooper, which tended to make some of the more important aspects of Lewis's life seem less important, and that of William Griffin, who failed to write about new material that he had discovered (116). Another critic explains that even though Wilson had not had the personal acquaintance with Lewis that previous biographers had, he does a good job with his "detailed, intimate knowledge of two major factors in Lewis's life—Oxford University and English literature" (Aeschliman 54). Yet another critic of Wilson's book is not so generous with praise. Gilbert Meilaender believes that the best biography of Lewis is the one by George Sayer and that Wilson's book is full of puzzling judgments that he has "pondered several times but remain[s] unable to fathom" (525).

One agreement among the critics is that the book seems to have been written in haste. Brookhiser notes that some parts of the book that Wilson thought to be most important are not explained well and are therefore hard to understand (62). Another critic also noticed signs of haste when it became apparent that Wilson only mentions Lewis's most powerful book twice, which made it seem like Wilson was in a hurry to finish, causing serious oversights (Meilaender 525).

Two critics state a specific problem with the tone. Brookhiser says that "too often his tone, which is meant to be conversational, slides into chattiness" (62). Another critic found Wilson's book enjoyable to read, but felt that his tone often becomes "snide and condescending" and that "very few people are mentioned without that tone of voice creeping through" (Meilander 528).

Believability is the major area of concern that troubles the critics. Riga explains that Wilson's ideas are highly speculative and that he takes many risks in these speculations that "seem ill-advised or just plain wrong" (116). Another critic also mentions Wilson's theories about Lewis's personal life (Elson A3). Riga states that these arguable judgments made about Lewis in Wilson's biography will lead readers to question the validity of the book (116).

There are also other faults in the biography that cause them to question its validity. Meilaender explains that what is unique about Wilson's book is that he attempts to analyze the psyche of Lewis, but that Wilson also fails to support his ideas with sufficient factual evidence. When talking about the way that Wilson analyzes Lewis in search for an understanding of him and his relationships with women, the critic explains that the evidence used to support his ideas "can't carry the interpretive load Wilson places upon it. The threads form an informative and witty narrative, but the facts do not fully persuade" (528).

Brookhiser says that there is a problem with Wilson's point of view. Wilson writes that the most attractive Lewis is the author of *English Literature in the Sixteenth Century*. Brookhiser disagrees sharply with him and says that "that book, like all of Lewis's criticism, is as fresh and sharp as Wilson says it is; but to be attracted to it primarily is like focusing on Mozart as a Mason, or Sir Arthur Conan Doyle as a table-rapper" (62).

Overall, the critics agree that the book is lively, readable, witty, and pleasurable to read. However, the more convincing critics are the ones who see past this and realize that there are many faults in Wilson's book that cannot be overlooked. These critics seem to be more educated in the life of Lewis and offer more information to support their claims. They do not agree with the illogical way that Wilson attaches so much significance to events in Lewis's life in order to demystify his personal life and beliefs. "The longer one ponders Wilson's narrative, the more difficult it becomes to grasp its logic" (Meilaender 528).

Works Cited

Aeschliman, M. D. "Getting the Core." Rev. of *C. S. Lewis: A Biography*, by A. N. Wilson. *National Review* 30 April 1990: 52–57.

"Beer and Beatitudes." Rev. of *C. S. Lewis: A Biography*, by A. N. Wilson. *The Economist* 3 March 1990: 81.

Brookhiser, Richard. "Seeking Faith." Rev. of *C. S. Lewis: A Biography*, by A. N. Wilson. *Commentary* May 1990: 61–62.

Elson, John. "Love's Labor." Rev. of *C. S. Lewis: A Biography*, by A. N. Wilson. *Time* 5 March 1990: A3.

Meilaender, Gilbert. "Psychoanalyzing C. S. Lewis." Rev. of *C. S. Lewis: A Biography*, by A. N. Wilson. *Christian Century* 16 May 1990: 525–529.

Riga, F. P. Rev. of *C. S. Lewis: A Biography*, by A. N. Wilson. *Choice* September 1990: 116.

Throughout her revision process, Melody had kept returning to her original sources, selecting new quotes to replace some she had already used and using what she had written as a way of checking on what she had read. At the same time, the revisions kept refining what she was saying, helping her to discover new associations of ideas and to sort through the material she had already assembled in order to present it more logically and more clearly. At that point she also goes back to the photocopied reviews and the information she has assembled about them to generate her "Works Cited" listing in conjunction with the handbook assigned to the course. This is the presentation text she turns in.

Working at Wordsmithery

The process that a composition goes through may vary from fairly straightforward and sequential to bewilderingly convoluted, but the undeniable evidence of the testimony and texts of wordsmiths

of all kinds is that success at wordsmithery grows out of commitment, effort, and time and can be fostered by an awareness of a
range of strategies adapted to the needs of the project-in-progress.
As these samples show, the final draft emerges out of a process of
engaging ideas in written language, a process that is usually un-
predictable in the ways language and thought interact with one
another to produce drafts and texts but a process that nonetheless
you can direct and influence by understanding how they interact.
Writers who know these things and make allowances for them are
better able to appreciate their work and, consequently, better able
to become accomplished at wordsmithery.

REFERENCES

Bell, Elizabeth. "The Magic Circle." *Writers on Writing*. Vol. II. Ed. Tom Waldrep. New York: Random House, 1988. 3–10.

Bereiter, Carl. "Development in Writing." *Cognitive Processes in Writing*. Ed. Lee W. Gregg and Erwin R. Steinberg. Hillsdale: Lawrence Erlbaum, 1980. 73–93.

Couture, Barbara, and Jone Rymer. "Interactive Writing on the Job: Definitions and Implications of 'Collaboration'." *Writing in the Business Professions*. Ed. Myra Kogen. Urbana: NCTE, 1989. 73–93.

Croft, Mary. "Pablo, Go Home and Paint." *Writers on Writing*. Vol. II. Ed. Tom Waldrep. New York: Random House, 1988. 39–45.

Dillard, Annie. "How I Wrote the Moth Essay—and Why." *The Norton Sampler*. Ed. Thomas Cooley. 3rd ed. New York: W. W. Norton, 1985. 13–21.

Dillard, Annie. *The Writing Life*. New York: Harper & Row, 1989.

Dowst, Kenneth. "The Epistemic Approach." *Eight Approaches to Teaching Composition*. Ed. Timothy R. Donovan and Ben W. McClelland. Urbana: NCTE, 1980.

Gornick, Vivian. "An American Woman in Egypt." *They Went: The Art and Craft of Travel Writing*. Ed. William Zinsser. Boston: Houghton Mifflin, 1991. 101–120.

Jerome, John. *The Writing Trade: A Year in the Life*. New York: Viking, 1992.

Leas, Connie. Personal interview. 15 Sep. 1986.

Lorch, Sue. "Confessions of a Former Sailor." *Writers on Writing.* Vol. I. Ed. Tom Waldrep. New York: Random House, 1985. 165–171.

Maimon, Elaine P. "The Voices of a Writer's Mind." *Writers on Writing.* Vol. II. Ed. Tom Waldrep. New York: Random House, 1988. 137–144.

McPhee, John. *The John McPhee Reader.* Ed. William Howarth. New York: Vintage, 1977.

Murray, Donald M. "One Writer's Secrets." *College Composition and Communication* 37 (May 1986): 146–153.

Murray, Donald M. *Shoptalk.* Portsmouth, NH: Boynton/Cook—Heinemann, 1990.

Nykamp, Susan. Personal interview. 15 Dec. 1982.

Olson, Sigurd. *Songs of the North.* Ed. Howard Frank Mosher. New York: Penguin, 1987.

Phelps, Louise Wetherbee. "Rhythm and Pattern in a Composing Life." *Writers on Writing.* Vol. I. Ed. Tom Waldrep. New York: Random House, 1985. 241–257.

Plimpton, George, ed. *The Writer's Chapbook.* New York: Viking, 1989.

Polanyi, Michael. *Personal Knowledge: Towards a Post-Critical Philosophy.* Chicago: University of Chicago Press, 1968.

Primeau, Ronald N. *Writing in the Margins: From Annotation to Critical Essay.* New York: McKay, 1976.

Reeves, Richard. Personal interview. 8 Nov. 1984.

Root, Robert L., Jr. *Working at Writing: Columnists and Critics Composing.* Carbondale: Southern Illinois University Press, 1991.

Schneebaum, Tobias. "A Drive Into the Unknown." *They Went: The Art and Craft of Travel Writing.* Ed. William Zinsser. Boston: Houghton Mifflin, 1991. 141–165.

Schuster, Charles I. "Richard Selzer and John McPhee: A Contrastive Analysis of the Composing Process." Annual Conference of National Council of Teachers of English. San Antonio, 22 Nov. 1986.

Sommers, Nancy. "Between the Drafts." *College Composition and Communication* 43:1 (February 1992): 23–31.

Steinbeck, John. *Working Days: The Journal of "The Grapes of Wrath."* Ed. Robert DeMott. New York: Penguin, 1990.

Thoreau, Henry David. *The Journal of Henry D. Thoreau*. Ed. Bradford Torrey and Francis H. Allen. Boston: Houghton Mifflin, 1906.

Warnock, Tilly. "How I Write." *Writers on Writing*. Vol. I. Ed. Tom Waldrep. New York: Random House, 1985. 305–315.

White, E. B. *The Letters of E. B. White*. Ed. Dorothy Romano Guth. New York: Harper & Row, 1976.

Wicker, Tom. Personal interview. 8 Oct. 1982.

Woolf, Virginia. *A Writer's Diary*. Ed. Leonard Woolf. New York: Harcourt, Brace, 1954.

Zwiger, Ann, and Edwin Way Teale. *A Conscious Stillness: Two Naturalists on Thoreau's Rivers*. New York: Harper & Row, 1982.

Credit Acknowledgments

Guizzetti, Mari, L. Journal Entry 7. February 18, 1991. Reprinted by permission of the author.

Jerome, John. *The Writing Trade.* From *The Writing Trade* by John Jerome. Copyright © 1992 by John Jerome. Used by permission of Viking Penguin, a division of Penguin Books USA Inc.

Kerr, Walter. Notes for review of *Ghosts.* Reprinted by permission of the author.

Lundeen, Scott. "How I Gained Self-Confidence Through Water-Skiing" (two drafts). Reprinted by permission of the author.

Powser, Heather C. Reading log on Jane Tompkins. March 30, 1992. Reprinted by permission of the author.

Rees, Brian T. "Ink's Barber Shop" (prewriting including mapping, listing, clustering; rough draft; journal entry on work in progress; and final draft). Reprinted by permission of the author.

Sagorski, Melody, K. Composition Journal Entry 9: A Speculation on Revision (Part II) and "A Report on Critical Reviews of *C. S. Lewis: A Biography*" (multiple drafts of research paper). Reprinted by permission of the author.

Wargelin, Stacey E. Writing log. January 29, 1990. Reprinted by permission of the author.

INDEX

A

Abstracts, 27–28
Annotations, 28–29

B

Bell, Elizabeth, on importance of
    clean copy, 110–111
Bereiter, Carl, constraints on
    writing, 7
Blake William, marginalia on
    Reynolds, 28

C

Clustering, 48–49, 50, 122–124
Commonplace books, 30–31
Comparison of experienced
    wordsmith and beginning
    wordsmiths, 12–15
Composing processes, 10–12, 14,
    71–72, 79–80
    compared with preparation of
        presentation text, 110–113
    examples of work carried
        through, 122–137
    See also Drafting; Going

public; Revising; Starting;
    String-saving
Conversation, 54–55, 95
    for starting, 54–55
    for revising, 95
Croft, Mary, 21, 44–45, 48
    on rehearsing, 44–45
    on segmenting, 48
    on string-saving, 21

D

Darwin, Charles, notebooks of,
    17
DaVinci, Leonardo, notebooks
    of, 17
Denby, David, on drafting, 65
Diagrams, 49, 51–52, 53, 122–123
Dialectical notebooks, 26–27
Dillard, Annie, 19–20, 63–64,
    74–75, 82, 85, 98
    channelled composing, 74–75
    discovery draft, 63–64
    "How I Wrote the Moth Essay,"
        19–20, 63-64, 85, 98
    on outlining the draft for
        revising, 85

Z

Zero drafts, 55–56, 63–64, 68,
        85–90, 93, 125–126,
        131–132
    examples of, 85–90, 125–126,
        131–132
    See also Discovery drafts

Z